The YAT Language of New Orleans

THE YAT LANGUAGE

OF

NEW ORLEANS

THE WHO DAT NATION

The True Story – How it all Began

By

Ray Canatella

iUniverse, Inc.
Bloomington

The YAT Language of New Orleans
THE WHO DAT NATION / The true Story - How It All Began

iUniverse books may be ordered through booksellers or by contacting:

iUniverse
1663 Liberty Drive
Bloomington, IN 47403
www.iuniverse.com
1-800-Authors (1-800-288-4677)

ISBN: 978-1-4620-3282-2 (pbk)
ISBN: 978-1-4620-3295-2 (ebk)

Printed in the United States of America

iUniverse rev. date: 07/19/2011

Dedicated in loving memory to my wife Margaret
who encouraged me to create this book
And to my three wonderful children
Terry Canatella Jeanfreau
Raymond S. Canatella
Derek R. Canatella
who wanted to know all about the YAT language
and how it got the name

PLUS

All the wonderful people who call New Orleans
their home and everyone else around this country
who were forced to leave because of Hurricane Katrina

In addition, a very special thanks to

My son Derek Canatella who created my book cover

Nancy Brister for allowing me to use photos from her site

and

Benny Grunch for allowing me to mention him and his

very funny YAT songs that he performs for all to enjoy.

INTRODUCTION

This book is more than just a record of the New Orleans "YAT" language. It was written to provide the true history as well as the background of why New Orleans speech and dialect came to be known as the YAT language and how it all began. Is the YAT language exclusively a product of New Orleans? Without question it certainly is. The name "YAT" which is used to describe the way most of the people who were born and raised in New Orleans speak definitely began here in our great city by the Mississippi river. Many people have written about the New Orleans YAT language, but so far no one has ever mentioned the "true" reason why the name YAT actually came to be applied to our New Orleans speech. The main reason for that is because not many writers that wrote about the YAT language never bothered to speak to someone who lived through the era when it all began. Let me say right here that the complete true story of how our New Orleans speech and dialect came to be known as YAT, began way back in the 1930's, 40's, and 50's which some people in the 21st century might consider ancient history. Of course in the very beginning it wasn't called YAT. The word YAT is a name that evolved through three decades and then came into existence in the early 1960's. In this book, I will explain the "true" story of what happened in New Orleans that brought about the name YAT to describe our unique speech pattern and pronunciation of words. It all started in the 9th Ward in our great city and then began to spread throughout downtown, then uptown. Why did it become popular throughout the United states and many parts of the world? Well, it was because THE NEW ORLEANS SAINTS football team and their loyal fans created the WHO DAT NATION by using the YAT idioms, or should I say it was the specialized vocabulary the Saints fans used when they would yell, "WHO DAT SAY DA GONNA BEAT DEM SAINTS, WHO DAT, WHO DAT."

CHAPTER ONE

In this publication, I will try to make the incomprehensible sounds uttered by the New Orleans locals, understandable and appreciated. If you are a tourist and you are new in town, you won't have to embarrass yourself by asking a local, "Are you from Brooklyn?" In addition, you won't have to be afraid if someone points to you and asks, "Do you mind if I "ax" you about my city before you mispronounce the name?"

Before we get into the words we call the YAT language, I would like to tell you a little bit about the city of New Orleans, which is unique in many ways. In fact the city is so unique, that before we get into the YAT dictionary, I want to explain certain cultural traits and peculiarities about our city, going back to the very beginning. So distinctive are these traits that they do not exist in any other city in the country.

1

To begin with, everyone knows that New Orleans is a city that is located in the southern part of our country. However, it is not a southern city. And of course not everyone knows that the people born and raised in our city do not speak with a southern accent. As a matter of fact, it irritates most New Orleans residents when a Hollywood producer decides to make a movie about our city and create characters that speak with a southern drawl. If only they would take the time to do a little research by coming to New Orleans and spending a little time here and listen to the average local speak, they would then get it right. Moreover, it doesn't matter what nationality a person is, Black White, or Brown, if they grew up in our city, they will have an accent that is compared to New York, the Bronx, Brooklyn and in some parts of New Jersey, or other cities in the northeast. How it all came about is not hard to explain.

At one time New Orleans was one of the largest seaports in the country next to New York. Just as people from the different countries around the world entered the United States by way of New York's Ellis Island, they were also entering our country through New Orleans, even though we didn't have anything as elaborate as an Ellis Island here. Therefore, because of the many different cultures entering New Orleans from around the

2

world, it became a cosmopolitan city just like New York. As the immigrants from Ireland, Italy, France, Germany, Spain and many other countries too numerous to mention, learned to speak English, their pronunciation, or style of expression began to filter down to the children, going as far back as the late 1700's.

Now New Orleans may be the most written about city in all of America. Yet, very few studies have been made that tried to overlook both the "Magnolia and moonlight" romantic view, and maybe something more critical, because it bewilders and constantly confounds the preconceptions of our city. New Orleans is semi-tropical in climate, lush in its setting, exotic in architecture, sensual and somewhat hedonistic in atmosphere and yet worldly because it is and always has been a bustling seaport. The very name of our city seems to evoke romance and myth. No wonder then that most writers continue to perpetuate old myths and create new ones. What they do is miss the true uniqueness of New Orleans, a city where no city should be, yet has been a remarkable successful city for a very long time.

From 1718 until 1810, New Orleans was essentially European in its physical shape and design and in human orientation. However, both France and Spain were unable to hold on to New Orleans as part of an empire against the Americans that were flooding into the Mississippi Valley after 1800. Once the Louisiana Purchase removed the political barriers to the development of New Orleans' natural economic and situation advantages, it brought population growth as well as economic development. From 1803 until 1861, our city population increased from 8000 to nearly 170,000. The 1810 census revealed a population of 10,000 making New Orleans the fifth largest city in the United States after New York, Boston, Philadelphia and Baltimore. However, because of its location, New Orleans, from 1810 until 1840, grew faster than any other American city. What is interesting about its growth is that by 1830, New Orleans became the third largest city in the nation. behind New York and Baltimore. Back then, we were considered a little big city. Of course, right before Hurricane Katrina, New Orleans had dropped down to only the 31st largest city in the country. Yet, even though it became a somewhat smaller city, New Orleans is still considered one of the top places to visit by people from around the world. Why? Well. Not only because of the Mardi Gras, but because of the food, the culture and many things too numerous to mention right here.

Now let me get back to our accents and speech patterns. What is interesting to note, that although a New Orleans resident will pretty much speak with a New York accent, there appears to be variations in pronunciation and grammar, depending on what part of the city they come from. Sort of what happens in the different boroughs in New York. People in Brooklyn speak a little different than the residents of the Bronx, or Queens, or any other section of New York. Of course, after the advent of television, there were a lot of changes in the way words were pronounced, not just in New Orleans, but all around the country. It seemed that a lot of locals began to copy the speech that they heard on TV. Of course, not everyone did. The pronunciations and speech patterns of most of the people down in the 7th and 9th Ward continued to sound like they were from Brooklyn, or the Bronx. In the early days, it may have seemed odd to a tourist back then to hear someone from uptown sounding slightly different from someone who grew up in the downtown part of the city, or even someone from across the river. It's still New Orleans, yet they sounded different.

BEFORE WE GET TO THE YAT DICTIONARY

THE SECTION BELOW IS FOR OUR WONDERFUL

TOURISTS

HOPEFULLY IT WILL HELP THEM UNDERSTAND

NEW ORLEANS A LITTLE BIT BETTER.
5

There are some locals who might tell you that the highest point in New Orleans is Monkey Hill. We can explain why the Irish Channel is not a TV program about the Gaelic-language. Our burial plots are six feet above ground, not six feet under. We can show you where Tchoupitoulas Street (Chop-a-tool-as) is located, but who can spell it? You are not to worry when we show you a ship riding higher in the river than our houses. We are not talking about Israel, or the Middle East when we talk about the West Bank. When we talk about a shop on Magazine, we are not talking about a periodical. If you get on a bus, marked cemetery, you need not be afraid. On a hot day, we can take you to a sno-ball shop and treat you to a sno-ball that comes in twenty-five to eighty delicious flavors.

While in New Orleans, you will be able to eat a "Lucky Dog" that's not somebody's pet, or "Drink a Hurricane" without being blown away. If we talk about a po-boy, it's not about some poor guy who does not have any money, but a great tasting French bread sandwich. If someone takes you to a crawfish boil, don't get upset if they tell you, "Be careful not to eat the dead ones and you need to suck da heads, and pinch da tails to really enjoy the crawfish." When we were growing up our parents would take us to the park to go on the "chute da chute" and we never heard of a slide. While we were at the park, everyone loved to ride the "Flying Horses" which could have been the Merry-go-round and no one ever spoke of a carousel. We have no idea what a dragonfly is, but we have thousands of mosquito hawks all over our city. If you go to one of our Mardi Gras parades, it's possible that you could leave with footprints on your hand if you are not careful. We can also explain why a lot of us have a parade ladder in our shed. While in New Orleans, don't ever make plans to rent a room at Hotel Dieu. We can explain to you why the color purple was associated with K & B drugstores, and not a movie. We use to play hopscotch on "da bank-it" when we were kids, using a piece of slate. Even though slate is not found in this part of the country, we have had so much slate brought in from France in the 1700's, that almost all of the older houses built in New Orleans have their roofs covered with slate which is practically Hurricane proof. Then, if we tell you we like "Tipitina," we are not talking about giving a tip to a waitress named Tina. Also, no tourist should ever leave our fun city without listing to the musical sounds created by "Benny Grunch and the Bunch," a very clever and well known singer and entertainer who performs our New Orleans Yat musical favorite songs. Such as, "The Twelve Yats of Christmas / Santa and his reindeer used to live here / Ain't no place to pee on Mardi Gras day / Ain't

7

dere no More / Christmas in Chalmette / just to name a few. If you can't find Benny Grunch's songs locally, just go to Amazon.com, they will have his CD's, you won't be sorry.

ABOVE ALL ELSE, WE LOVE TO SAY:

"Only in New Orleans!" or, "It's a New Orleans thing."

NOW, MORE ABOUT OUR CITY

Most cities across the country will have direction such as North, South, East and West. This would not work in New Orleans. If you were to asking for directions to go somewhere, you would be told it was uptown, or downtown, or on the riverside, or lakeside, or on the west bank. Actually, if you had a compass with you, you might as well put it away. South Rampart will take you towards the north, while on North Rampart you will be going towards the south. Furthermore, if you got on the ferry to crossed the river to go to the West Bank, you would actually be traveling south.

I would also like to mention at this time, that all of the different groups of people settling in New Orleans, gave the city the type of food that now exists today. The French, Italians, Africans, Indians, Germans, Spanish,

Jews, Filipinos, Slovaks and many others, all contributed to the creation of some of the tastiest meals known to man, "Creole Cooking." Our food is so unique and delicious, that French chefs from Paris and other parts of France come to New Orleans just to learn the method of creating the meals that are commonplace in our city. In addition, many chefs from around this country still travel to New Orleans just to learn Creole cooking.

While I'm on the subject of cooking, we need to set the record straight about Creole cooking in New Orleans. It has been and always will be different from Cajun cooking. I mention this, because too many people around this country think that they are the same, mainly because of the different chefs that get on television to cook and call some Creole dishes Cajun. Creole cooking was created in New Orleans by a diverse group of nationalities such as the French from France, the Spaniard from Spain, the Africans from Africa and the Indians who came from across Lake Pontchartrain. These were the main groups of people who, over the years, eventually added to the development of the now famous Gumbos and other fine Creole dishes. Now, the delicious Cajun cooking, although famous throughout the country, was developed by the French who came from Canada, the Germans and some of the Spanish who settled in the area of Louisiana called Acadia.

New Orleans remains a city with strong character and a fascinating history involving the French Quarter, the music, the riverboats, haunted houses, monkey hill, Mardi Gras, Po' boy sandwiches, Italian Muffuletta and many other wonderful things I could continue talking about in this book. However, this book is about the YAT language, as well as how it all began. So, read on and enjoy the YAT language from the Who Dat Nation.

I would like to mention here, before we get into the actual history and dictionary, of what the "YAT" language really means. For the most part, it is the way New Orleanians like to pronounce their words. Furthermore, because the word "YAT" began with the slang used by the "Cats" in the "Cat and Frat," or should I say the "DOO WOP" era from the 1950's, I'll including a lot of the slang words that were used back then. Some of those words are obsolete in today's world; however, a lot of them are still around. ENJOY.

CHAPTER TWO

THE YAT LANGUAGE

To begin with, how did the word YAT come to be used to describe the idiom, or speech pattern that is used in New Orleans to define our language? Well, it didn't just happen all of a sudden. It evolved from another part of the country with groups of men (and some women) who created a type of suit that became popular way back in the late thirties.

THAT SOUNDS ODD DOESN'T IT?

How could the creation of a particular type of suit have anything to do with a style of speech and dialect that we call YAT that is used in New Orleans? Well, read on and you will then understand the true reason of how it happened, once it is explained to you in detail. The famous popular suit that started it all was called the ZOOT SUIT.

Zoot Suit (occasionally spelled **Zuit Suit**) is a suit with high wasted pants, wide-legs, that has an extreme taper from the knee down to a very small-cuffed bottom. The suit has a long coat with wide lapels and wide padded shoulders. Often Zoot suitors wore a felt hat and pointy French style shoes that came in black and white and many bright color combinations. In addition, Zoot suits usually featured a gold watch chain that dangles from the belt to the knee, or below, then back up to a side pocket. The suits also came in as many bright colors as you could imagine. (If you Google "zoot suit", you will be able to see pictures of the actual suits on line. This style of clothing was popularized by African-Americans, Mexican-Americans, Puerto Ricans, Italian-Americans and Philippine-Americans, during the late 1930's and early 1940.s. In England, during the 1950's, the bright colored Zoot-Suits with wide velvet lapels were worn by a group of tough kids, called the Teddy Boys.

In the beginning, Zoot suits were for special occasions, such as a dance, or a birthday party. Some of the Zoot suits were single-breasted "HEPCAT" high fashion suits, while others were called "TOPCAT" Zoot suits. In addition, anyone wearing a Zoot suit was occasionally called a "COOL CAT." (Now, remember those three words, Hepcat, Topcat and Cool Cat). The suit first gained popularity in the Harlem Jazz culture in the late 1930's and early 1940's where they were initially called "drapes". The amount of material and tailoring required, made them luxury items, so much so, that the U. S. War Department issued a statement during the early 1940's, saying that they wasted material that should be devoted to the World War II effort. This extravagance during wartime was a factor in the "Zoot Suit Riots" in Los Angeles between the Mexicans (who were also known as Pachuco) and the servicemen stationed there. The riots were a major factor in influencing young men around the country mainly because of all the radio news stations broadcasting the incident. By adopting that style of clothing and wearing the oversized suits was a declaration of freedom and self-determination and even somewhat rebellious.

In New Orleans, the younger generation who were not in any college fraternity, began dressing up in the bright colored Zoot suits to go to dances, parties, weddings and any other place they wanted to look and feel good about themselves.

In New Orleans, young men and teenagers shared the fascination about Zoot suits just as they did in other cities around the country. The younger generation, if they could afford them, bought and wore the Zoot suits to go out in the evenings. It appeared that the bright colored clothes and the "Pachuco Slang" developed by the Mexicans from Los Angeles, seemed to spread everywhere the Zoot suits became popular. The older generation began to consider any one who wore a Zoot suit and talked with a Pachuco style slang, rebellious. Then of course, the suit, the slang, the attitude and the image, all came together.

If you didn't use the slang when talking to the neighborhood teenager, you were considered a "Square". If you did use the slang, you were considered "cool". This went on throughout the 1940's. It could have been because of the Los Angeles riots or maybe not, no one knows for sure. However, the term Pachuco was being used in a negative connotation that came along with the wearing of a Zoot suit. The public began to associate anyone wearing a Zoot suit and calling themselves Pachuco, were considered troublemakers. This was the beginning of the end for Zoot suit wearers in New Orleans, even though there were some who still wore

14

Zoot suits. However, it was the beginning of the "CAT" and "FRAT" era in our city as well as other cities around the country.

In the 1950's when rock and roll was born, the Zoot suits were being phased out by the teenagers in New Orleans. However, the kids who were calling themselves the Cats, did adopt a lot of the Pachuco styles, such as the distinctive haircuts resembling a ducktail, better known as a "DA". The haircut was left full on top and it was then greased with Vaseline, so it could be combed from each side to the center which created a curl that came down in front by the forehead. Then we had the "Balboa" cut which was a type of haircut that was cut short on the top and long on the sides, that was greased also, so the hair could be combed back into a "DA". I would like to mention here that the so called "Cats" in other parts of the country, were being called Greasers. That movie Grease was made to highlight the teenagers who were considered Cats in New Orleans and Greasers elsewhere.

The New Orleans Cats also adopted the baggy pants that were pegged at the bottom, but not with all the bright colors like the Zoot suits. Most of the Cats wore black peg pants and bright colored shirts with a high collar they called a "Mr. B" collar. If for some reason, they were not wearing a shirt with a "Mr. B" collar, then they would put

15

their shirt collars up. This was an indication they were "CAT". Earlier, we mentioned the Zoot suit wearers were called "Hepcat, Topcat, or Cool-Cat," well the New Orleans teenagers decided to use only the term "CAT" because they didn't want to be associated with Pachucos or Zoot suit wearers because that denoted troublemakers to the general public. However, they did want to indicate they were different from the "Frats" who were High School Seniors or College kids belonging to a fraternity.

The Frats for the most part, wore ordinary street clothes and their hair was usually cut short so they wouldn't have to comb it too often, or not at all. They also wore white buck shoes, which gave them more of a "Pat Boone" clean cut look. Meanwhile the Cats were wearing black shoes with white soles that were called Continentals. When the song "Blue Suede Shoes" came out, the Cats began wearing Blue Suede Shoes.

CHAPTER THREE

§-NOW WE WILL LEARN THE REAL REASON HOW

THE WORD "YAT" CAME INTO EXISTANCE TO

DISCRIBE THE WAY NEW ORLEANIANS SPEAK- §

If a guy was walking along the sidewalk, or "Banquette" (pronounced "bank-it") and he had his shirt collar up and a group of teenager Cats were passing him in their car, they would lean out of the window and yell "Where y'at Cat!" He would respond in one of three ways. He might yell back with, "Aw rite. Where y'at," or he would yell "I'm cool dude" and wave, or he might yell, "I ain't nowhere, man" even though they didn't know one another, they all had a camaraderie, meaning they were in tune with one another. Cats wouldn't always use "Cat" at the end of their response. In the beginning of the Cat and Frat era, the greetings would always be "Where y'at Cat." Then, just as the term Pachuco and Zoot suit had been used in a negative connotation, the term "Cat" followed. In another words, "Cat" became associated with "bad teenagers" because of the way they dressed. To the older population, they appeared to be outside of the mainstream hard working nicely dressed Frats. However, in reality, being a "Cat" didn't mean they were not hard workers, or didn't go to school, because they did do everything the Frats did, accept dress in the normal fashion of the day. Back then, the grown-ups, in and around New Orleans, as well as in other parts of the country, couldn't identify with the "Cats" or the way they dressed and talked. Therefore, they began to associate young "Cats" with bad people just as they did with the Pachuco and Zoot suit wearers. Especially since the adult population hated "rock and roll" (DOO WOP) music the Cats loved, which began to take over the airwaves in the early 1950's. To them, that music was the work of the devil himself. The news would show a DJ breaking his records and vowing never to play rock and roll music again. A Radio stations had camera crews come out to their building, to film a bulldozer rolling over and crushing all rock and roll records.

18

Any incident like that was cheered by the adult population. They were trying to convince everyone in America that the only good music was from the 1930's or 1940's. Why? Well, the 1950's music was Doo Wop music and it was associated with the "Cats." It was the same in other parts of the country; there Cats were known as "Greasers." Little did the adult population of the day realize that they were going to get old, just like their music. When Elvis, Chuck Berry, Fats Domino, Little Richard, as well as all the other rock and roll and Doo Wop singers, came along, the adult population, had to put-up with the music they seem to hate. Little did they know that the music from the 1950's and 1960's would one day, be considered some of the greatest dancing and listening music ever recorded in our history, accept for maybe the great long haired classics of the 16th and 17th century.

Somewhere between the 1950's and early 1960's, the "Cat era" had completely ended. However, the greetings between most people in New Orleans continued to use the term "Where y'at." Below are a few lines of a song that was written about the Cat's greeting.

♫"It's not hello, or how are you,

or anything such as that.

In New Orleans when friends are seen

we all say where y'at."♫

It is without a doubt that the teenagers, who were "Cats" in the early 1950"s and 1960's grew up and continued to use "Where y'at" to greet someone. Therefore,, the word "YAT" to describe the New Orleans form of language was born.

As we mentioned earlier, the New Orleans pronunciations of words were labeled YAT because it was a fun way to describe how New Orleanians spoke. However, the "Cats" of long ago were using certain slang words to describe many different things. So, in this dictionary I will give you those slang word and then tell you what it means in everyday English. Some of those words are still used today, while many are not. All New Orleans words and the way the locals mispronounce them will be classified as "YAT" speak. The words will be spelled out to indicate how they are pronounced by a large portion of the population. Then, the YAT word will be used in a sentence, which will give you a better understanding of what the word means. After all, most of the people who were born and raised in our great city do pretty much, speak alike with slight different inflections in the way the words are pronounced. Of course, there will always be those who do not speak "YAT," or mispronounce normal English words. For the most part, we still have the "Frat" element here in New Orleans. We must never forget that our wonderful colleges such as Tulane, Loyola, and Dillard, plus all the other universities with their fraternities that are located here will always be the pride of our great city. After all, young kids come to our colleges and universities from all parts of our country. Nevertheless, it is very possible that there are a lot of "Frats" that will use YAT words just because many of them are fun words.

CHAPTER FOUR

As you read earlier, the older generation of the 1950's and 1960's hated the local Cats because of the way they spoke, or the way they dressed and their "Doo-Wop" and rock and roll music. So, eventually the teenage Cats gave up part of their greeting, which was "Where y'at Cat?" That was mainly because they felt persecuted for dressing up with peg pants, bright colored shirts with their collars up, wearing continental shoes, plus playing their brand of Doo Wop and rock and roll music and calling one another Cat, (or Cool Cat). So, all the New Orleans Cats decided to begin greeting one another without using the word Cat in order to fit in with the older folks. The local greeting then became. "Where y'at." That greeting soon began to spread all over the city and outlying areas. Wherever teenagers lived or worked, the older generation would constantly hear "Where y'at, man," or "Where y'at Steven," (or some other name), to greet a friend or co-worker. That greeting soon became acceptable all over the city and outlying areas.

Now you know how the word "YAT" came into existence to describe our New Orleans speech and pronunciations of words. Without a doubt it was definitely derived from the 1950's New Orleans Cats greeting, "Where y'at Cat?" What's interesting is that the older generation who hated the "Cool Cats," (or Hep Cats) their greetings and their music, could not wipe out either the music or the type of greeting that eventually evolved into "Where y'at," which has lasted for well over 60 years and is still around today.

In the 1950's and 1960's many of the older folks back then, were predicting that the future generations in our city as well as around the country would look back and would considered the clothes, (Peg pants, poodle skirts and hair do's), the speech and the Doo-Wop music, to be the absolute the worst decades in musical history. Yet, the Doo-Wop and rock and roll music in today's world is considered by everyone (young and old), as some of the most beautiful "Golden Oldies" music ever recorded. So much so, that Time-Life and others are re-mastering the songs done by singers and groups, so they

23

can sell the Doo-Wop music for a small fortune through one hour commercials on TV. They run those commercials very often, so they must be selling a lot of those Golden Oldies CD's. I am positive they wouldn't be spending their money on TV commercials if they weren't making money from the sales.

Actually looking back to the 50's and early 60's I can honestly say that it turned out to be a great time to be alive. What I would like you to do right now is stroll back with me and go back.....before the internet, or Super Nintendo.....before drive by shootings, or aids, or herpes, long before semi-automatics and crack.....way back when life was a lot simpler.

I'm talking about sitting on the curb or sitting on the stoop until late in the summer evening just to catch a breeze and it was safe to do so. All the neighborhood kids would play hide-and-go-seek, or Simon says, while others would play Red-light-Green light. How about having metal skates that needed a key to put it on your foot. Then there was hopscotch and jump rope, playing with the hula hoop, marbles, tops, or flying a kite to see who could get theirs to go higher than anyone else. Does anyone remember when a quarter was considered a decent allowance, or reaching into the gutter for a penny, or running through the sprinklers if you passed a house that had grass in front of their home? How about going to the grocery and buying sunflower seeds, a box of raisins, wax lips and mustaches and penny candy. And let's not forget that coke came in glass bottles, even out of the coke machines and they were never broken in the street even in the so called bad neighborhoods.

That's not all either. No one ever complained because we didn't have air condition, because no one ever considered that it even existed. Yet it was still a good time to live. Even when it took five minutes for the television to warm up and mom made you turn it off when a storm was coming. Also, let's not forget there were only three TV stations you could watch, yet watching TV was a lot of fun, there was The Mickey Mouse Club, Rocky and Bullwinkle, kookla, Fran and Ollie, Spin and Marty, Nancy Drew, the Hardy Boys, Laurel & Hardy, Howdy Doody, The Peanut Gallery, The Shadow Knows, Roy Rogers and Dale with Trigger, and who can forget The Lone Ranger, or Superman. No one will ever forget Dick Clark's American Bandstand, Jackie Gleason and of course all in black and white and you actually had to get up off the sofa or chair to change the channel and no one ever complained.

Let's not forget when nearly everyone's mom was home when us kids arrived home from school. Some kids had lunch boxes with a thermos with chocolate milk, or Kool-Aid. No one fussed because you ate Kool-Aid powder with sugar from the palm of your hand, because it wasn't going to make you fat or become a diabetic. How about when some kids would actually go home for lunch without telling the teacher.

LET'S KEEP GOING BACK!

When it was very rare when someone owned a pure bred dog, especially in New Orleans. When mom wore nylons that came in two pieces. When all male teachers swore neckties and female teachers had their hair done almost every day and wore high heels. How about making paper chains at Christmas, or silhouettes of Lincoln and Washington around their birthday. At school there was the smell of paste and pencil sharpener dust, because we all had to keep our pencils sharp. We didn't have ball point pens back then and a fountain pen was used only on special occasions. And the worst thing you could do at school would be to flunk a test, or worse yet, getting caught chewing gum. But there may have been something the older kids were doing that was even worse. That was getting caught smoking in the school bathroom. Not because smoking was bad for them, it was because they were too young to be smoking. Which reminds me, no one ever had to fear for their life because of drive by shootings, drugs, or gangs, it was being sent to the principal's office and then being sent home to get additional punishment from your parents.

At the end of the high school year, if you were about to graduate, the prom was in the gym and at some schools, there was a live band to dance to and at other schools the kids danced to a juke box with some great Doo-Wop songs. Most of the girls wore those fluffy pastel gowns, or poodle skirts and the boys wore suits for the first time and everyone was allowed to stay out until 12 midnight.

Remember back then there were only two types of sneakers, Ked and PF Flyers and the only time they were worn was in gym. How about the girls who had to wear those ugly gym uniforms.

When going downtown seemed like you were going somewhere special. Canal street was the only place you could shop for clothes, shoes or toys at Woolworths 5 & 10 stores, or Sears and Roebuck. Climbing trees, making forts out of apple crates, back yard shows, lemonade stands, playing cops and robbers, cowboys and Indians, or laying down with a friend and trying to figure out what each cloud look liked.

How about kids jumping on the bed and maybe having a pillow fights, walking to the neighborhood show (Movie Theater), and running until you were out of breath, or laughing so hard your stomach would hurt. Then no one would dare step on a crack or you'd break your mother's back. How about summers that were filled with bike rides, baseball games in the street, going **bowling, or visits to the swimming pool. Then the best of** all we would go out to Pontchartrain Beach to go on all the rides, like the Zephyr, the Laugh in the Dark, or the Ferris wheel.

Remember when laundry detergent had a free drinking glass, dishes, or a towel hidden inside the box. How about when stuff from the store came without safety caps and hermetic seals, because no one had yet tried to poison a perfect stranger.

How about when the '57 Chevy was everyone's dream car. Cruising was a sport, peeling out, or laying rubber. Drag races late at night on roads that were seldom used, or taking your favorite girl to the submarine races out at the lake, or driving out to City Park and taking her to the Mona Lisa lover's lane, which was a lot more private than the lake fronts lover's lane. Remember when everyone from all over the city would meet at Wallace and Raoul's restaurant's parking lot to decide on where we were going to drag race that night. And for some reason, there was always a motorcycle policeman waiting for us to leave so he could follow us and he could then call in for reinforcement to "bust us" that night. Or on other occasions, there would be a "rat fink plant" in our group who would drop a nickel on us to let the police know in what area we were going to drag racing. I said a nickel, because at that time, the pay phones in New Orleans would only cost a nickel, even though in other cities, to make a phone call, it would cost a dime.

If you were going out to the beach with friends, you made everyone put up a quarter for gas, which was only 24¢ a gallon, and you didn't have to put any more gas in your car until the following week. No one ever cared about gas mileage, because it seemed like you could drive for ever on a couple of gallons. When you drove into a gas station, to get 50¢ worth of gas, you got your windshield cleaned, your oil checked and you didn't have to get out of your car, because the gas station attendant would pump your gas for you and your tires were checked for air, without asking and all for free. Some gas stations even gave trading stamps and if you filled a book, you could get a nice gift. Back then new cars off the showroom floor was selling for a whopping $1500. dollars, so we would all look around for a good used car that sold for around $50. to $150. dollars and the only thing wrong with it was maybe you would have to buy a battery or put new brake shoes on the car, which you could do yourself if you were handy with tools. If the car belonged to your parents, and you wanted to use it, you didn't have to ask them where the keys were, because they were always in the car.....in the ignition and the door was never locked

Speaking of that, you would get in big trouble if you accidently locked the door at your house, since no one ever had a key. Actually when I was growing up, on Burgundy Street, we had a lot of side doors on the driveway side, that couldn't be locked, because there weren't any locks on them.

THOSE WERE THE DAYS MY FRIEND, WE THOUGHT THEY WOULD NEVER END

Now that you had a peek into the heart and soul of what made us locals tick, in and around our great city of New Orleans and why the word YAT is part of our local speech, I will in the next chapter, offer you our lexicon of local speech, visitors will not have to secretly wonder, "What in the hell is he/she talking about?"

I hope that what was read above brought back memories for all the New Orleans natives and I hope that it will also enlighten our visitors to our wonderful Crescent City by the river. It may help make the difference between a mere tourist and a truly interested visitor. We don't want a visitor saying "Huh?", when after they order their sandwich and the lady behind the counter ask them, "Ya want dat dressed, dawlin'?"

CHAPTER FIVE

A LEXICON OF NEW ORLEANS

TERMINOLOGYAND SPEECH

THE YAT DICTIONARY

ABSOID

> **Translation:** Absurd. "Dat was de most absoid ting I ever hoid."

ACE

> **Translation:** One dollar "Slip me an Ace Gate." (Let me have a dollar.)

AIR-CHECK

> **Translation:** Recording a song. "I like dat song. I'm gonna air-check it for later."

ALGERIAN

Translation: Someone who lives in Algiers, a part of the city of New Orleans that lies across the river, (called the West Bank)

ALLIGATOR

Translation: Anyone avoiding work. "He's just an alligator lyin' in da sun."

ALLIGATOR PEAR

Translation: Avocado. A tropical pear-shape fruit with a green skin.

ALOIT

Translation: Alert. "Der police told us to be aloit while in dis neighborhood."

ANYWAYS

Translation: Besides. "Anyways, I don't care what happened to dat Cat."

ARABIAN

Translation: Someone from Arabi, a community located in St. Bernard Parish.

AWRITE

    Translation: All right. A response to the greeting, "Where y'at?" Also another response: ain't no ware man." Or, "I'm cool dude."

AW

    Translation: Are. "Aw ya sure dis is der rite address?"

AW, WHAT

    Translation: Placed at the end of a question. "Ya gonna finish dat sandwich aw what?"

AX

    Translation: Ask "What do ya want to ax me about?"

BABY

    Translation: A term of endearment. (For either sex.) "Say baby, I got some bread to spend let's go downtown and shake it tonight."

BABE

    Translation: Short for baby. "Hurry up babe it's gettin' late."

BACKATOWN

    Translation: Many years ago, down in the 7th

and 9th ward where part of the city that was
located on the other side of North Claiborne Ave.
going out towards the lake it was considered
"Backatown."

BAD

Translation: Good. "Dat dude is a bad ass
player."

BAG

Translation: Enjoyment – fun "Ya ax me if I
play pool? You bet. Dat's ma bag."

BALL

Translation: To enjoy. "I'm havin' a ball now
and I'm ready to ball tonight."

BALLOON LUNGS

Translation: Singer with a great voice. "Dat Cat
has balloon lungs, he can hold dat note for a very
long time."

BANK-IT

Translation: Sidewalk. This word is use mostly
in New Orleans. The French spells it "Banquette"
meaning, a raised platform, sidewalk, or a ledge.

BARN BURNER
　　Translation: Hot girl. "Ma chick is a real barn burner."

BAWROE
　　Translation: Borrow. "I needda bawroe ya cawh (car) tonight."

BATTA
　　Translation: Cake Batter. "I gotta mix dat batta so I can make ma boitday cake."

BAT'TROOM
　　Translation: A room in the house where there are no bats, but where one bathes.

BEAT
　　Translation: Exhausted. "Boy, I'm beat. We've been giggin' all night."

BEAUCOUP
　　Translation: Plenty. Pronounced "BooKoo" Used a lot in New Orleans. "Man, ya gonna be in beaucoup trouble if ya don't do your homework."

BEDDA

    Translation: Better. "We bedda not be late for ya mamma's boitday party."

BERL

    Translation: Boil. To create hot water. "I needda berl a few eggs."

BIN

    Translation: Been. "I couldn't go because I bin sick."

BINHAVIN

    Translation: A Longtime owner. "She's binhavin' dat dress forever."

BINLOOKIN

    Translation: Searching. "I've binlookin for dat book a long time."

BIRDBRAIN

    Translation: Stupid. Someone with a brain the size of a BB.

BLOW YA TOP

    Translation: Getting angry. "Hey, don't blow ya top, I'll be dare (there) soon!"

37

BOBO

    Translation: A small injury, or wound.

BOID

    Translation: Bird. "I gotta feed da boids before I go."

BOINT

    Translation: Burned. 'If ya play wit dem matches, ya might get boint."

BOINTS DA BOARD

    Translation: Burn the plank. This saying is equal to the modern saying such as "Written in Stone."

The saying goes way back to the Pirate days, when a Pirate Captain gave his men a specific order to do, or not do something, causing the men on board to refer to the order as being burned in the plank, which meant that what the captain ordered, the men knew it could not be changed for fear of life or limb. In downtown New Orleans, where many pirates lived in the early 1800's, such as Jean Laffite and some members of his crew, that saying was probably passed down from some of their descendants. Of course after a hundred or so years, that saying "Burn the plank," without a doubt became corrupted because of the way the 7th ward and 9th ward people spoke, so the saying became "Boints da board." And was used in card games. Once you put a card down, you could not change your mind and pick it up to place another one down. If you tried to do that, someone would yell, "Boints da board." That would of course remind you that you couldn't change your mind once you played a card. Hopefully I explained the saying enough to be understood. Incidentally, anyone reading the above explanation and doubt it, should get a copy of the book titled "A DICTIONARY OF SLANG & UNCONVENTIONAL ENGLISH (Eight addition, published by MacMillan Publishing Company) Page160

BOITDAY
> **Translation:** Birthday. "I bedda get somethin' for her boitday."

BOO
> **Translation:** A term of endearment. "Hey, boo come gimme a hug."

BOOGIE

> **Translation:** Dance. "Say baby, let's go boogie tonight."

BRA

> **Translation:** To address some man you hardly know. "Say bra, what time is it?"

BREAD

> **Translation:** Money. "Ya gotta come up wit da bread if ya wanna buy ma caw."

BREAK TAG

> **Translation:** An inspection sticker for your caw. (car)

BRING DOWN

> **Translation:** Unhappy. "Let's cut out. Dis is a bring down place for me."

BRO

> **Translation:** The same as "Bra," but is actually short for brother. Also used to address someone you hardly know. "Hey bro where y'at?"

BROAD

> **Translation:** A good looking young woman.

40

"Dat broad is a real knockout."

BUCKS
    Translation: Dollar bills. "I had eight bucks left after I paid da bill."

BUD
    Translation: Short for friend or buddy. "Hey, bud how ya bin?"

BUG
    Translation: Annoy. "He really bug's me."

BUMMA
    Translation: Bomber. That meant bad news during world war II, especially in Europe, when bombers flew over their targets to drop bombs.

BURGUNDY
    Translation: A street in New Orleans that is pronounced "Bur-GUN-de" unlike the wine which is spelled the same way, but pronounced "BUR- gandy." The reason why the people of New Orleans pronounce the street "Bur-GUN-de, is because the street was named after a province in France with the same name.

41

BUZZED

>**Translation:** Feeling dizzy. "Last night, at da dance, I got buzzed."

BY MY

>**Translation:** At my. In New Orleans, people like to say – "I'll be by my house until noon if you wanna come over." Used instead of, "at" my house.

CABBAGE

>**Translation:** Money. "Hey, I got enough cabbage to pay for our plane ticket."

CAL-LEE-OPE

>**Translation:** Calliope. A street in uptown New Orleans that the locals pronounce Cal-lee-ope, yet when they mention the organ with the same name on the riverboat Natchez, they call it a "Ka-LIE-o-pee." This is the correct way. "Go figure."

CANARY

>**Translation:** A female singer. "I like da way dat canary sings."

CAP

>**Translation:** Mister "Hey, cap can ya tell me

what time it is."

CARBURATOR TROUBLE
Translation: Can't move fast. "How is dat horse gonna win da race, when every time he runs; he has carburetor trouble?"

CARNIVAL TIME
Translation: Another name the locals use when they talk about Mardi Gras.

CATLICK
Translation: Catholic. "There aw a lotta Catlicks' in New Orleans."

CAT
Translation: A hip dude, or cool dude. "Man dat Cat gets all dem women."

CATCHA
Translation: Meet with you. "I gotta go now, but I'll catcha later."

CAUSE
Translation: Because. "She went out wit him cause he was nice lookin'."

CAWFEE

Translation: Coffee. A very hot brew that people all over the world love to drink.

CAW

Translation: Car. "When didja get that nice looking caw?"

CAWD

Translation: Card. "She paid wit her credit cawed cause she had no cash."

CHALMATION

Translation: A fun way to call someone from Chalmette. A city in St. Bernard Parish or as a lot of people like to call it, "Da Parish."

CHARACTER

Translation: Unusual. "He soitanly was a character."

CHARM-IN

Translation: Beautiful. "Dat goil over dare is very charmin."

CHAW'MA

Translation: Charmer. "I could not resist that

broad, she was a real chaw'ma."

CHICK
  Translation: Girl. "I'd like to meet dat chick she's charmin.

CHIEF
  Translation: Someone you look up to. "Tanks chief ya were a big help."

CHIRP
  Translation: Sing. "Dat canary really knows how to chirp."

CHOPS
  Translation: Teeth. "I'm goin' to da dentist to get ma chops cleaned."

CLAM
  Translation: Shut up. "Dose bad kids clam up as soon as I walk in da room."

CLOAK ROOM
  Translation: Clothes closet. Back in the 1700's,

right through to the 1800's, many New Orleans people wore "cloaks" instead of coats, especially in the French part of the city. They would hang clothes in the cloak room. The term was used until the 1940's, especially in public schools located in downtown New Orleans.

COLD

Translation: Without emotion. "You mean she slapped him in da face and just walked out wit out tellin' him why? Dat was really cold man."

COM'ON

Translation: Latch on, or be with someone. "She keeps tryin' to com'on to him, but he just didn't care for her."

COMBO

Translation: Ham and cheese po-boy sandwich. "Gimmie a combo dressed. Lettuce, tomatoes, mynez and don't forget da pickles."

COOKIES

Translation: Records, disks (CD's & DVD's) "Dat DJ played some cool cookies last night, lots of Doo-Wop oldies but goodies."

COOL
> **Translation:** Great. "Dat dude is a real cool Cat."

COPAFEEL
> **Translation:** To touch. "When he got close to her, I saw him copafeel."

COPASETIC
> **Translation:** Acceptable, or satisfactory. "Tings are really copasetic around here."

CRAZY
> **Translation:** Interesting. "Listen to dat crazy beat da band is layin' on us."

CRIB
> **Translation:** Apartment. "Hey babe, let's go to ma crib and have a drink."

CUT
> **Translation:** To leave. "Hey man, let's cut, I'm tired of dis place."

CUT OUT
> **Translation:** Sneak off. "I had no idea she was

gonna cut out on me after we had dat argument."

DA

Translation: The. "Da whole city went nuts when da Saints won da Super Bowl. All ya hoid after dat was, "WHO DAT SAY DA GONNA BEAT DEM SAINTS. WHO DAT? WHO DAT?"

D-A

Translation: Ducktail. A hairstyle in which the hair is swept back at the sides then met in an upturned point in the back. Worn by the Cats in the 1950's.

DA HOUSE

Translation: Fat girl. "She has a pretty face, but da house is just too big for me."

DADDY-O

Translation: Addressing someone, you like. "Where ya't daddy-o."

DARE

Translation: There. "Listen ta ya!" "Dare ya go again. Witcha smart mouth."

48

DARK

Translation: Angry or upset. "He was in a dark mood when he hoid da bad news."

DAT

Translation: That. "Who dat say dey gonna beat dem Saints?" "Who dat?" "Who dat?"

DEY

Translation: They. "Tell me why dey ain't gonna go to da game."

DAWLIN

Translation: Darling. "Dawlin, you want some desert now?" Used a lot by waitresses in New Orleans.

DE

Translation: The. (same as "da.")

DEAD MAN'S LIGHT

Translation: An overhead light at a secret location in City Park that the Cats would drive their car under to reach a lover's lane called Mona Lisa.

DEM

Translation: Them. "Are ya sure we can trust dem goils to show up?"

DESE

Translation: These. "I sure hope dese tourist loin to love our city."

DIDJA

Translation: Did you. "Didja see dat crazy dude crash into dat fence?"

DIG

Translation: Understand. "Do ya dig what I'm sayin'?

DINEROS

Translation: Dollars. "I bet fifty dineros on dat horse and he came in last. I know what happened, he had carburetor trouble. What a bumma."

DIMWIT

Translation: Stupid. "What a dimwit he toined out to be."

DIS

Translation: This. "Dis place is really jumpin' tonight."

DODO

Translation: Sleep. "You look tired child, let's go make dodo." Take the French saying "Fais dodo," (To dance until you are tired, then you will need to rest or sleep.

DOGIN'

Translation: To irritate. "She said that Cat was dogin her all night."

DOLL

Translation: Pretty Girl. "Dey got some cute dolls goin' to dat club."

DOZE

Translation: Those. "Doze people were de woist dancers I ever saw."

DRAPES

Translation: Suit of clothes. "Man, I really dig that Cat's drapes."

DONCHA

   Translation: Don't you. "Look man, if ya gotta get up oiley, why doncha leave now."

DONNA ROAD

   Translation: To travel south on a highway. "Dat place is donna road a little ways."

DOUBLOON

   Translation: A large coin minted on a yearly basis by various Mardi Gras krewes, to be thrown from the parade floats.

DOUGH

   Translation: Money. "Before we leave tell me how much dough ya got witcha?"

DOWN BY LAW

   Translation: Respectful. "The woik he did was "down by law."

DRAG

   Translation: Depressing. "It's really a drag being around dat guy."

DRESSED

Translation: Lettuce, tomatoes, pickles and mayonnaise. "Gimme a po-boy dressed and hold da pickles.

DRIVE

Translation: Ambition. "Dat guy has a lot of drive."

DRIVES

Translation: Tough to bargain with. "Dat Cat drives a hard bargain."

DUDE

Translation: A man. "Dat dude could run as fast as a deer."

DUKES

Translation: Hands. "He had his dukes full while handlin' dat crowd."

EARL

Translation: Oil for cooking. "I'll fry dem ersters as soon as da earl gets hot."

ELLESHOO

Translation: LSU - Louisiana State University.

53

ER'ANGE

   Translation: Orange. "Ya mamma, can peel dat er'ange pretty fast."

ERL STATION

   Translation: Oil station / Gas Station. "I gotta stop at da erl station and get gas."

ERSTERS

   Translation: Oysters. "Everyone likes to eat dem ersters fried or raw on da half-shell."

FERL

   Translation: Foil. "Don't throw dat away, just wrap it in ferl for tomorrow."

FLIPPED

   Translation: Upset. "I really flipped when she told me no."

FLIPPED HER LID

   Translation: Angry. "She flipped her lid when she lost her poyse." (Purse)

FLOIT

   Translation: Flirt. "He got embarrassed when she began to floit wit him."

54

FLY CHICK

    Translation: Listening. "Not so loud man, dat fly chick over dare is tryin' to hear what we aw talkin' about." (Similar to the fly on the wall)

FLYIN' HORSE

    Translation: A merry-go-round, or a carousel. "A term used only in New Orleans."

FOIST

    Translation: First. "I remember the foist time I met her."

FOR

    Translation: A preposition used by New Orleanians instead of "at" or "by" when referring to time. "Da parade is for 7 o'clock, but we bedda get dare for six if we wanna find a parkin' place." (This one tends to be particularly confusing to non-natives.)

FORGETCHA

    Translation: Forget you. "How many times do I hafta tell ya just forgetcha ever met dat crazy broad."

FRACTURE

Translation: Effect. (Usually humorously) "Man your jokes fracture me."

FRAIL

Translation: A slim young lady. "Man, dig dat frail how skinny she looks."

F'SHOW

Translation: For sure. "Are you telling me dat really happened, f'show?"

F'TRUE

Translation: When used as a question, it means "Is that so?" or "Ya kiddin." **"Ya mean dat really happened f'true?"**

GAWD

Translation: God. "Gawd only knows I did da best I could."

GIGGIN'

Translation: Dancing. "Let's go giggin' tonight."

GIMMIE

Translation: Give me. "Gimmie dat drink before ya spill it."

GIMME SOME SKIN
>   **Translation:** Shake hands. "Hey man, long time no see, gimme some skin."

GLIMMERS
>   **Translation:** Eyes. "Dat frail has beautiful glimmers."

GO CUP
>   **Translation:** A paper cup for drinking alcohol while walking on the streets in New Orleans. Bottles and cans are illegal.

GOIL
>   **Translation:** Girl. "Every goil I go out wit wanna dance da Jamaican, so I had to loin how, aw I would lose out on gettin' another date."

GRIP
>   **Translation:** Suitcase. "Da cab is here. Don't forgetcha grip."

GRIS-GRIS
>   **Translation:** A voodoo spell. Pronounced (GREE - GREE). There are locals as well as tourists, who go to a Voodoo lady to have a curse put on someone.

57

HAFTA

    Translation: Have to. "I hafta catch a plane to New York tomorrow."

HAMBOYGER

    Translation: Hamburger. "One of the best hamboyger I ever ate was at Martins."

HAWT

    Translation: Heart. "She's got a good hawt."

HICKEY

    Translation: A knot on your head. "I hit ma head, and I wound up wit a hickey."

HIP

    Translation: In the know. "That Cat is one hip dude."

HISTREE

    Translation: History. "De histree of dis great city is amazin'."

HOID

    Translation: Heard. "I hoid the same story about dat Cat yesterday."

HOIT

Translation: Hurt. "I hoit all over after fallin' off der bike."

HOPSCOTCH

Translation: A game with ten numbered spaces drawn on the bank-it with a piece of chalk. A player would throw a piece of slate into one of the spaces then hop or jump on one foot to try and retrieve the piece without falling over. Then hop to the big round ten, turn and hop back .

HOT

Translation: A lovely person. "Wow, she's some hot chick."

HOW'S YA MAMMA AN' DEM

Translation: When someone is asking about your whole family, they will say, "How's ya mamma an dem?" (How's your mother and everyone else.)

ICEBOIG

Translation: Iceberg. "Dose old ships had to be careful not to hit an iceboig."

I'LL TAKE ME.....

Translation: I'll "have" me. "Say sweetie, I'll

59

take me a piece of dat pie now."

IMMA
> **Translation:** I am going to. "Imma leave now, but will catcha later."

IN DER MIX
> **Translation:** With us. "Wit dat Cat in der mix, we can't fail."

INTOYPERTATION
> **Translation:** Interpretation. "His intoypertation of what really happened didn't make any sense."

IRISH CHANNEL
> **Translation:** A section of the city that once was inhabited by Irish immigrants.

JAMAICAN
> **Translation:** A dance created by the Cats during the 1950's to replace the jitterbug dance of the 1940's. Some of the moves are very similar.

JAMMIN
> **Translation:** Exciting. "Dat band was jammin' last night."

JAM SESSION
    Translation: A spontaneous get together after
    hours, in the French Quarter.

JAWN
    Translation: John. A popular boy's name and
    what a bathroom is called.

JITTERBUG
    Translation: A 1940's jittery swing dance.

JIVE TURKEY
    Translation: A smart-ass guy. "Dat jive turkey
    don't fool me nun."

JOIK
    Translation: Jerk. "What a joik he toined out to
    be."

JOIMS
    Translation: Germs. "Ma mamma told me, if I
    don't kill all the joims by washing ma hands, dey
    soitanly will kill me."

JOINT
    Translation: Nightclub. "Dat joint toined out to
    be a nice place."

61

JUMPIN

> **Translation:** To have a good time. "Dat joint was jumpin' last night."

KAPUTS

> **Translation:** Breakdown. "De udder day I was drivin' out by de lake and all of a sudden my motor went kuputs and it wouldn't start for nutin.'"

K&B PURPLE

> **Translation:** A particular shade of deep purple. Well known if you grew up in New Orleans. "He was so mad his face toined K&B Purple.

KERL

> **Translation:** Coil. "My caw wouldn't start because da kerl boint out."

KERN

> **Translation:** Coin. "Ya mamma had only two quarters in her kern poyse."

KICKS

> **Translation:** Pleasure., or enjoy. "I get my kicks when I listen to dat comedian."

KICK DA CAN

Translation: Made known. "Once he kicked da can, everything was exposed."

KILL ME

Translation: Absolutely enjoy. "Man, ya really kill me wit dem crazy jokes."

KILL IT

Translation: Stop. "Hey man, I don't like dat song, kill it.

KING CAKE

Translation: A special type of cake made with a little baby doll in it, during the Mardi Gras season and used when we have a King Cake Party.

KING KONG JUICE

Translation: Cheap moonshine. "Hey man, I scored some King Kong Juice from Mississippi. Aw you Cats ready to get buzzed aw what?"

LAGNIAPPE

Translation: Pronounced "LAN'YAP" An old New Orleans custom of giving you something extra when you buy a product from a store. For instance, if you bought a dozen doughnuts from a bakery, they would give you thirteen just for shopping at their bakery. That lagniappe was to encourage you to come back again.

LATCHED ON

Translation: Wanted to be with. "Dat chic latched on to him cause he was spendin' heavy."

LETCHA

Translation: Let you. "I'm gonna letcha come with me, but ya betta behave."

LINCOLN

Translation: Five-dollar bill. "I'm almost broke. I only got one Lincoln left."

LOCKA

Translation: Locker. Where you hang your clothes. The word was used in place of closet.

LOIN

Translation: Learn. "When is dat kid gonna loin to behave when we go out?"

LOLLYGAG

Translation: Waste Time. "What a lazy bum. He

likes to lollygag too much."

LOOKA

Translation: Come see. "Wow, looka here man, your tire is goin' flat."

LOOKIT

Translation: Watch. "You can only lookit TV after you finish your homework."

LOOT

Translation: Money. "She had a poyse full of loot, yet she wouldn't loan me a dime."

LOWUH NINT

Translation: Lower ninth, as well as the ninth ward which is located in downtown New Orleans. Without a doubt, this is the area of the city where the idiom YAT to describe our New Orleans speech, originated.

MA

Translation: My. "Ma whole life flashed before me when I got hit by dat caw."

MAIN SQUEEZE

Translation: Favorite girlfriend. "Hey man, I

65

wancha to meet my main squeeze."

MAKE GROCERIES
Translation: To go grocery shopping. It is possible that the expression may have originated with the French expression for grocery shopping. "faire le marché", which means in English "Do the market" or "Make the market." Later, market was changed to groceries.

MANY MOONS AGO
Translation: A long time ago. (Indian lingo.) "We stayed at dat hotel many moons ago."

MARDI GRAS
Translation: Same as Carnival time in New Orleans.

MAW-MAW
Translation: Grandmother. "Ya maw-maw makes a fantastic gumbo yeah."

METREE
Translation: Metairie. A community in Jefferson Parish called Metree by locals and Met-TAIR-ee by the tourist. The correct way is Met-air-ie.

66

MICKEY MOUSE

Translation: Cheap. "Ya couldn't afford a good one, so ya went out and bought a Mickey Mouse lookin 'piece of furniture like dat?"

MOYCHANDIZE

Translation: Merchandise. "Dat store seem to be selling nutin' but cheap moychandize."

THE MONA LISA

Translation: A secret lover's lane in City Park that was more private than the lake front lover's lane. The New Orleans Cats would drive their car past dead man's light into a wooded area where it was very dark. Most downtown Cats knew about "The Mona Lisa" and where it was located. It got its name because of her secret smile that was stated in the song that was sung by Nat King Cole, which was very popular at the time.

MONKEY HILL

Translation: A large hill that was built in Audubon Park during the depression by the WPA workers, so kids could go upon it and have fun riding their bikes down it, because there are no hills in New Orleans. Now everyone has fun calling Monkey Hill the highest point the city.

MONKEY WIT

Translation: Play with. "Don't monkey wit doze wires. Ya might get shocked!"

MOOLA

Translation: Money. "I can't go witcha tonight, I'm outta moola."

MOYDER

Translation: Murder. "I tell ya, it was moyder drivin' in dat storm."

MOYSEE

Translation: Mercy. "Everyone in New Orleans was at da moysee of Hurricane Katrina."

MUFFULETTA

Translation: Pronounced muff-a-letta, (NOT muff-a-lotta!) A new Orleans Italian sandwich created by the Italians at Central Grocery in da Quarter.

MYNEZ

Translation: Mayonnaise. A favorite dressing used on sandwiches in and around New Orleans.

NAMBY-PAMBY

Translation: Spineless. "Her new boyfriend seems very manly. Nutin like dat namby-pamby guy she used to date."

NEEDDA

Translation: Need to. "Dat's a cute chick, I needda get up da noive to go and ax her for a date."

NEUTRAL GROUND

Translation: The grassy, or cement strip located in the middle of a wide street. The words "median" or "island" are never used in New Orleans. If you use one of those foreign terms instead of "neutral ground," it is a dead giveaway that you're not from around here, or anywhere close.

NEW ORLEANS

Translation: Pronounced New Or-le-ans, NOT New Or-leeen, accept in a song. Some like to say Nawlns, just to try and be funny.

NOIVE

Translation: Nerve. "He had de noive to ask her out again."

69

NOYCE

    Translation: Nurse. "She was dat pretty noyce I met at "Hotel Dieu."

NUN

    Translation: None "I asked a lotta dem goils to go out wit him, but nun would go."

A-NUDDA

    Translation: Another. "Dat's funny, I saw a-nudda Cat wit da same shoit a little while ago. Him and his goil were goin' in da show."

NUTIN

    Translation: Nothing. "She said she didn't want nutin to do wit him."

NUTTINONIT

    Translation: A sandwich that's not dressed. It only contains the main ingredient.

OILEY

    Translation: Early. "Sometimes I gotta get up oiley so I can get to woik on time."

ON DA WES' BANK

    Translation: On the west bank. The other side of

70

the Mississippi river, which is due South of New Orleans not West. (Try and figure that one out.)

OUT TO LUNCH
Translation: Absent minded. "Every time I try to explain somthin' to him, he seemed to be out to lunch."

OVA BY
Translation: Over by. A replacement for the prepositions "at" and "to" when referring to someone's house or destination in general. "Where ya goin' tonight?" "Ova by ma mamma's house."

PA'KORN
Translation: Pecan. A nut indigenous to the south and loved in New Orleans, as an ingredient in pies and pralines. It is pronounced pee-can elsewhere.

PAD
Translation: Same as crib. "Some of dose Cats will be jammin' at my pad tonight."

PARISH
Translation: County. Louisiana is the only state

within the United States of America that does not have their administrative territorial subdivision called county. This happened when the U.S. purchased the Louisiana territory from France. Our state was allowed to continue to use the "Napoleonic Law" that existed at the time of the sale.

PARRAIN

Translation: French for Godfather. Pronounced "PAH-ran." "Ma parrain came to visit me de udder day."

PASS BY

Translation: To stop at someone's house to visit. It does not mean to drive by in your car and keep going. "I'm gonna pass by ya house tomorrow. Just tell me what time ya gonna be dare?"

PAWK

Translation: Park. "While at Audubon pawk I'll go see Monkey Hill and maybe ride my bike down from de high pernt."

PERNT

Translation: Point. "What's the pernt of comin' to New Orleans, if ya not gonna have fun."

PLANT YOU NOW
AND DIG YOU LATER

Translation: When you plan to meet someone later. "Hey, Cat, imma plant you now and dig ya later." Other goodbyes that were used by the Cats. "I'm leavin' Steven." "I gotta go Joe." "See ya later alligator." Sometimes a response would be "After while crocodile!"

PO-BOY

Translation: Originally called "poor boy." A name given to the sandwich by the Martin Brothers during the 1930's depression. Around 1929, the streetcar motormen went on strike in New Orleans. Anytime one of the strikers came to their restaurant for something to eat, one of the brothers would say, "Here comes another poor boy for our sandwich." The Martin Brothers would give a free sandwich to him or anyone not working. That's how the po-boy sandwich got its name.

PODNA

Translation: Partner. "Hey podna come gimmie a hand wit dis box."

POIFECT

> **Translation:** Perfect. "She tried to become the poifect cook for him."

POYSON

> **Translation:** Person. "Dat poyson gave her the creeps de way he kept starin'."

POYCE

> **Translation:** Purse. "Whatcha got in dat poyse? It sure feels heavy."

PRALINE

> **Translation:** A sweet Creole candy invented in New Orleans. It is pronounced PRAH-leen, not PRAY-leen.

RI'CHUS

> **Translation:** Righteous. Someone you like after meeting them. "I found out he was a ri'chus Cat after I met him."

RITE

> **Translation:** Right. "The Saints aw gonna keep rite on winning."

74

ROCK AND ROLL

Translation: Music that was very popular during the 1950's.and early 1960's

RUG CUTTER

Translation: Swing dancer – Jitterbug. "Dat Cat is one cool rug cutter."

SACKBUTT

Translation: A woman with a big behind. "She's got a cute face, but I'm not sure I wanna date dat sackbutt.

SALTY

Translation: Smart. "That's one salty Cat. He seems to know everything."

SAMMICH

Translation: Sandwich. "If you wanted to get a great po'boy sammich in the city, back in der 1950's, den ya would go to the restaurant ware de po'boy was created which was Martin's on St. Claude street."

SCENE

Translation: A place. "Let's make da scene a dis nightclub tomorrow."

SCHWAGMANN'S BAG

Translation: A large paper bag used by the Schwagmann Brothers Giant Super Market which was enormous in which they packed your groceries in. The stores were located all over New Orleans before closing.

SENDS

Translation: A good feeling. "Man, dat chick really sends me."

SHARP

Translation: High Fashion. "He's one sharp Cat when he's dressed up."

SHEKELS

Translation: Dollars. How many shekels will I need to get in dat show?

SHELL ROAD

Translation: If the Cats wanted to frighten or punish someone, they would drive them out of the city on the pretext that they were going to a fun place. Once out on a dark lonely road, usually across the river, the driver would ask the intended victim to get out and check one of the back tires, because it may be going flat. When the victim got out of the car, the Cats would drive off leaving him on the dark road. They would leave him for about ten minutes, then come back and pick up a very frightened person. This was called "Shell Road," because originally this punishment was done on a shell road outside of the city.

SHOIT

Translation: Shirt. "Man, I dig that shoit ya mamma gave ya."

SHOOT-DA-CHUTE

Translation: A steep playground slide. Why the playground slides in New Orleans got to be named Shoot-da-Chute may be lost in history. However, Shoot-the-Shute is listed in the 2004 American Heritage College dictionary. It may be because the word chute describes a piece of equipment that was used to pour, or empty out something so it will slide down the chute, such as a coal chute that was used long ago when coal was delivered to houses because in cold weather our heat came from fireplaces.

SHORT

Translation: Car. "Dat Cat is driving a good looking short." (I have no idea how the name "short" got to be used to describe a car, but a lot of guys around New Orleans used it.)

SHOW

Translation: A movie theatre. True New Orleanians never say. "I went to da movie last night." They say. "I went to da show last night."

SHROUD-TAILOR

Translation: Undertaker. "Every time dat Cat dresses up in dat black suit, he reminds me of a shroud-tailor."

SINGLES

Translation: Dollar bills. "Hey dude, you got five singles for a Lincoln?" (A five)

SKIN ME

Translation: Handshake. "Where y'at Cat. Long time no see. Skin me man."

SMOKIN'

Translation: Playing well. "That Cat I was playin' pool wit last night was really smokin', lost every game."

SNAP YA CAP
   Translation: Same as "blow your top." "Calm
   down man, before ya snap ya cap."

SNO'BALL
   Translation: Snowball. A cup of finely crushed
   or shaved ice. It is then covered with your choice
   of many different flavors. The snowball machine
   was invented in New Orleans along with 50 or 60
   different flavors, unlike the snow cones that are
   sold everywhere else that have different colored
   syrups which all taste the same.

SOYKLE
   Translation: Circle. "When riding the flyin'
   horses at Audubon Pawk, all ya do is go around in
   soykles."

SOITANLY
   Translation: Certainly. "Pontchartrain beach
   was soitanly a fun place to go. Wit all dem fun
   rides like de Zephyr and de Laugh in da Dark, da
   Ferris Wheel and da entertainers such as Elvis
   comin' to da beach ta entertain us, what a treat.

79

SOLID

>**Translation:** Good or Great. "Ya gonna like him, he's solid."

SOYVIN

>**Translation:** Serving. "Dat waitress was soyvin me a very delicious meal"

SQUARE

>**Translation:** Not hip. "That Cat's a real square, he just can't dig what's happenin'. "

STRAIGHTS

>**Translation:** Cigarettes. "I gotta get me a pack of straights and some matches before I die."

STAWS

>**Translation:** Stars. "On a clear night, dem staws look beautiful in da sky."

SUBMARINE RACES

>**Translation:** When a Cat would meet a girl he liked, he would ask her if she would like to go with him to see the "submarine races." out by the lakefront. If she agreed to go, he would drive out to Lake Pontchartrain the lover's lane by the seawall and park. In the warm summer, they

would sit out on the seawall. They would look out over the lake while enjoying the cool breeze. When it started getting dark, they would then go sit in the car and wait for the races to start. They would then begin kissing and petting while they waited. After a while, the girl would ask the Cat. "When are the races going to start?" His response would be, as soon as they see the signal, which of course never came. If she wanted to leave because it was getting late, he would agree. He would then tell her that they probably postponed the races for that night, but they could then plan to come back at another time to see the races for sure. It was a great way to get a girl out to lover's lane. Even some of the Frats used that trick.

SUCK DA HEAD, SQUEEZ DA TAIL
Translation: Technique for eating boiled crawfish.

SUPOIB
Translation: "Superb. Dat was a supoyb performance she gave last night."

SUICIDE KNOB
Translation: Suicide knob was a spinning knob

that was placed on an automobile steering wheel, which was popular in the early 1950's. The driver could grab the "suicide knob" and turn a corner with one hand while having his arm around his girlfriend who was sitting close to him. Someone in the government decided it was too dangerous and outlawed it.

SUPA

> **Translation:** Super. "I gotta tell ya, dat dude we saw in dat movie look like he was built like supa-man aw sumptin."

SUMPTIN

> **Translation:** Something. "Dare was sumptin' I was gonna tell ya, now I forgot."

SUPOYB

> **Translation:** Superb. "When it comes to dancing, she is supoyb."

TANKS

> **Translation:** Thanks. "I didn't get any tanks for helpin' her wit da dishes."

TANKSGIVEN

> **Translation:** Thanksgiving. "After I eat on

tanksgiven, I gotta go lay down."

TAWK

Translation: Talk. "Dem Cats from Georgia sure tawk funny."

TERLET

Translation: Toilet. "After drinking six beers, he had to use the terlet."

TIDE

Translation: Tired. "I got sick and tide of her complanin,' so I left der scene before she drove me crazy."

TING

Translation: Thing. "Dat ting ya bought sure don't go wit our furniture."

TINK

Translation: Think. "I'm really tide after bein' out all night. Rite now I can't tink of anything but gettin' some sleep."

TOIKEY

Translation: Turkey. "Boy, I tink I ate too
83

much toikey at tanksgiven'."

TOIN

Translation: Turn. "He lost his toin when he stepped out of da line."

TOIMANATE

Translate: Terminate. "Dey decided to toimanate her last week."

TOOL

Translation: Easy to dupe. "That Cat is being used by doze goils; he's nutin but a tool."

TREE

Translation: Three. The number three, as pronounced by many locals.

TRILL

Translation: Thrill. "I found my trill on blueberry hill, is one of the great song by Fats Domino."

T'ROW

Translation: Throw. "You will always hear people yelling, "t'row me somtin' mister." at der parades on Mardi Gras."

84

UDDA

Translation: Other. "I was gonna call ya de udda day, but I got busy."

VEG'ER'TIBBLE

Translation: Vegetable. "Eat your veg'er'tibble soup or you can't go out."

VET-TRANS HIGHWAY

Translation: Veterans Highway. Located in Jefferson Parish. The locals call it VET-trans Highway and never give it a second thought.

VIOLATION

Translation: Violation is a fun way to call any person from Violet, Louisiana, which is located in St. Bernard Parish. Or as we like to say, "da Parish."

WANCHA

Translation: Want you. "When we go out tonight, I wancha to be cool."

WARE

Translation: Where. "Look, dares Johnny now." "Ware ya't Cat?"

WARE YA STAYIN' AT?

    Translation: Where do you live? "Since you moved back to da city, where ya stayin' at?"

WARE Y'AT?

    Translation: The traditional New Orleanians greeting and the source of the popular term YAT which began back in the 1950's and early 60's and is used to describe our New Orleans accent, even though we sound a lot like people from Brooklyn. The proper response to "Ware y'at?" is "Aw-rite," or "I ain't now are man." Or "I'm cool dude."

WIT

    Translation: With. "I had lots of fun wit dat goil when we went to da beach."

WITCHA

    Translation: With you. "Dat goil I saw witcha da other night was very charmin."

WITOUT

    Translation: Without. "She said she didn't wanna go to da show witout dressing up and lookin' pretty, so I hadda wait for dat goil for a-nudda half hour,"

WOIK

Translation: Work. "Every time I go to woik, dey make me stay and help dem other lazy goof offs, before I can leave.

WOILD

Translation: World. "Dat goil always claimed dat de woild is her erster."

WOISE

Translation: Worse. "Dat was da woise looking suit I ever did see."

WONCHA

Translation: Won't you. "Every time I come to pick ya up, woncha try and be ready to go, so we can get dare oiley."

WRENCH

Translation: Rinse. "You better wrench your hands after eating boiled crawfish."

Y'ALL

Translation: A shorter version of "all of you." However, in New Orleans, it is never spoken with a southern twang, or drawl.

YA

    Translation: You, or Your. "After ya wake up, go wrench ya face."

YA MAMMA

    Translation: Your mother. It seem to be a way of insulting someone who may have insulted you by accusing you of something you don't agree with, such as calling you a name. You would then come back with "ya mamma" this would in essence be accusing his mother of the same foul name or insult. (Sometimes it's in fun, sometimes it's fighting words.)

ZINK

    Translation: Sink. "After ya finish eatin' fried chicken, ya can wrench ya hands in da kitchen zink."

CHAPTER SIX

THIS PART OF THE Y'AT DICTIONARY IS CALLED LAGNIAPPE

Lagniappe (pronounced "Lan'yap,") is an old New Orleans custom of giving someone a little something extra even though it wasn't expected. The "extras" that I will mention in this chapter will be areas of interest that were exclusively New Orleans. Of course after they became so popular with tourists, many of them were adapted and used in other parts of the country.

However, we still have traditions and customs that are almost as old as the city itself, and can only be found, in and around our wonderful city. It would be impossible to cover everything that makes this city unique; nevertheless, I will cover some of the wonders of long ago and some that still exist today. Therefore, the younger generation and many of our wonderful tourists of today will be able to understand why New Orleans is so different from any other city in the United States. I will explain some of the facts that make this city such an interesting place to live, or just visit. After all, New Orleans is more than just the French Quarter, Bourbon Street, the music, or the Mardi Gras Celebrations.

After the Louisiana Purchase in 1803, the New Orleans' population began to increase rapidly from 8000 to 170,000. The 1810 census revealed a population of 10,000. making New Orleans the fifth largest city, after New York, Philadelphia, Boston, and Baltimore. Then, as a seaport and a major point of entry for our country, New Orleans grew at a faster rate than any other large city in America after 1810. By 1830, New Orleans then became America's third largest city. behind New York and Baltimore. We had the first operas performed in America and our fancy balls kept the numerous musicians fully employed. The local residents and tourists always enjoyed our cultural and recreational opportunities far beyond what most cities the size of New Orleans could ever offer.

Let's start with a tourist favorite, "St. Charles Streetcar Line."

"All ABOARD!" For a trip into New Orleans' past, on the oldest continuously operating streetcar line in the world. The first streetcars to run on steel rails were along Bowery St. in New York, in 1832. The second city in America to install streetcars was New Orleans, in 1835. Beginning in that year, all streetcars were pulled by horses or mules along steel tracks. One man in front drove the animals, controlled by a set of reigns. He had a break handle used for stopping the streetcar. A second man, called a conductor, rode in back. His job was to help passengers get on and off the streetcar, to collect

91

fares and give a signal to the driver when everyone was on board. The conductor gave the signal by pulling a rope that was attached to a bell in front.

Then around 1888, many cities began using electricity to operate their streetcars. A new name was soon developed for streetcars powered by electricity; they were called "Trolley Cars." However, the new name "Trolley Car" never caught on in New Orleans and streetcar is still used today. After 1888, the city began installing streetcar lines all over the city. No matter where you lived in the city, you never had to walk more than two blocks in any direction to catch a streetcar.

The photograph below was taken in 1895. As you can see there were hundreds of streetcars running on Canal Street alone, which is the main thoroughfare in the city. Canal Street was the dividing line between uptown and downtown. Before there was any such thing as a shopping mall, Canal Street was where everyone in the city had to go to shop for anything and everything, or even go to the movies. If you wanted clothes, shoes, toys, furniture, appliance for your kitchen, or buy music records, Canal Street was the only place you could go. And if you were shopping all day, and you got hungry, there were lunch counters in most of the department stores to feed you.

Up until the late 1940's it cost 7¢ to ride anywhere in the city and you never had to wait more than five minutes on Canal Street, or fifteen minutes anywhere else in the city. Furthermore, it did not matter what time of day or night it was, because the streetcars ran 24 hours a day. In the early 1960's, the city Council decided that the streetcars had to go. Fortunately, the St. Charles streetcar stayed. The St, Charles streetcar, that you ride today, still has mahogany seats, brass fittings and exposed ceiling light bulbs. Of course, they were installed long ago when plastic seats and aluminum railings didn't exist.

When the St. Charles Streetcar line began service in 1835, it was powered by steam engines. Afterwards, by horse or mule, then in 1893, the streetcars were electrified. Rolling along the "neutral grounds" on St. Charles and Carrollton Avenues for more than 175 years, symbolizes the charm and romance of our wonderful city.

Next on our list, is the Historic French Market, which has existed in the same location for over 230 years. Without question, the French Market is the oldest continuously operating public market in the United States. The area began as a Native American trading post on the banks of the mighty Mississippi River, and was the site chosen by the French Explorers for our great city. Since then, it has become a cultural, entertainment commercial and treasure, which New Orleanians proudly shares with the world.

Public markets once thrived in many parts of the United States. However, because public markets were very popular with the French who founded the city, New Orleans had more open-air markets than any other city in the country. This was long before we had corner groceries or super markets. Below are a few photographs of our Historic French Market in the early years.

This section of the French market above was taken around 1939 on Decatur Street.
Below is a close up of one of the fruit and vegetable stand located in the market.

Going back to the beginning, the French Market had many different sections that sold more than fruits and vegetables. There was the "Butcher Market Section" that sold meat from cows, goats, hogs and lambs. What is interesting, before refrigeration, the butchers would hang the meat on hooks over their stalls. When a customer wanted a steak, or a roast, or any other piece of meat, the Butcher would take down the meat, scrape off any surface that looked bad and cut off a fresh looking piece for the customer. (Why people didn't get sick is still a mystery. "Go figure.") It could be that when the meat was cooked, it killed all the germs. Another section of the French Market sold seafood caught in the river, Lake Pontchartrain and in the Gulf. The fish, crabs and shrimps sold, came to the market hourly, so they were continually fresh.

The picture below was taken around 1915. It shows how busy the French Market was back then. After all, if you needed food, the French Market was the only place in the city that you could get a variety of fruits, vegetables, meats and seafood.

Notice the streetcar tracks running along the center of

Decatur Street. People who didn't want to walk to the market could ride the streetcar there to do their shopping. Then, on the other side of the market, on Chartres Street, they could catch the streetcar to go home. Back in 1915, it only cost 5¢ each way to ride the cars.

The photo above is at one end of the French market that was taken somewhere between 1880 and 1897. Notice the horse drawn streetcar on the right.

Two more photos that were taken from the same angle, but in different years.

The picture below shows people bringing their baskets to do their daily shopping. There was no such thing as shopping bags for you to carry the groceries you bought back to your home.

The picture above is to show you how close to the river the French Market was built. The building on the left is the famous Pontalba Apartments, one of the oldest apartments in the country. The photo's lower part is Jackson Square; the year is 1864.

The Choctaw Indian squaws would come to the French Market from across Lake Pontchartrain and sit stoically on the curb, and offer to sell gumbo filé, which was a special powdered sassafras that was frequently used instead of okra to thicken the gumbo. They also sold other herbs and spices, in addition to baskets and pottery.

CHAPTER SEVEN

The selling of food and staples at the French Market was only part of how New Orleanians purchased what they needed. Each season had its special commodities that were sold. Early spring saw the arrival of strawberries and Japanese plumbs. Later, watermelon, dewberries, blackberries and figs became plentiful. Wild ducks, birds and other game were sold during the winter months.

Men and women who didn't have a stall in the French Market would become street vendors. Food vending on New Orleans streets is a custom as old as the city itself. Up until the 1940's, street peddlers covered just about every neighborhood in the city. Buying from those wandering merchants was extremely convenient for the homemakers. The prices were low, the products were of good quality, and it was always possible, after a bit of wrangling, to get something below the asking price.

Throughout the year, day in, day out, the street merchant's cries resounded throughout the neighborhoods of New Orleans. They attracted the people inside their homes by loudly singing what they had to offer. Most of these wonderful singsongs that was created by these vendors was so interesting, I decided to add a few of them here.

For instance, a vendor would stop his mule-drawn wagon in a neighborhood at a corner and cup his hand around his mouth, and begin yelling his song as loud as he could.

♫Watermelon! Watermelon! Red to the rind,

If you don't believe me jest open your blind!

I sell to the rich,

I sell to the po'

I'm gonna sell to da lady

Standing in the do'

Watermelon Lady!

Come git the watermelon that's fine

103

I say Lady, it's red to the rind!♫

In the wagon behind the vendor is a pile of green striped melons and besides him on the seat, is a melon cut in half to show it is "red to the rind." Despite that, the lady of the house would always demand that the vendor plugs the melon she happened to pick out, to prove it was ripe.

In another area of the city, an Italian vendor selling fruits and vegetable would sing using a little humor to attract attention.

♫Cantal--ope—ah

Fresh and fine

Just offa da vine,

Only a dime!

Lady, I have ah snap'ah beans

De nicest ya ever seen

I gotta corn and carrots by the peck

And fresh artichokes by the neck

104

Come and gettum lady! ♫

Throughout the city, the streets reverberated with their humorous and poetic cries. When it was blackberry season, you would be able to hear the street merchant sing, out as he walked around the neighborhood.

♫Blackber—reeeees! Fresh and fine.

I got blackber—reeeees, Lady! Fresh from the vine!

I got blackberries, Lady! Three glasses fo' a dime!

Blackberries. I got black—berreeeeeeeees!♫

When strawberries appeared preceding the blackberry season, peddlers, both white and black, both male and female, appeared all over the city. Even Sunday mornings resound with the cries of:

♫I got strawberries, Lady!

Strawberries fresh and fine,

I picked them myself off da vine.

Fifteen cents a basket

105

Two baskets for a quarter!

Come see my berries and we can barter♫

When the housewives would come out and gathered around the strawberry man's cart or wagon, they would peer into the small boxes of berries. Then they would begin inspecting carefully, always raising the top layer of the fruits, to see the ones underneath. It has always been a little "trick of the trade," which has been used even into modern times. Louisiana housewives have always been wise to the trick of putting the reddest and biggest berries on top and putting the small or green ones underneath.

From the very beginning of our city in the 1700's, "Street Vendors" could and would satisfy families by having practically anything they needed or wanted. For those that didn't want to, or couldn't make it to the French Market, they relied on the street vendors. If anyone wanted oysters, there was the Oyster Man crying out his singsong.

♫Oyster Man! Oyster Man!

Get your fresh oysters from the Oyster Man!

Bring out your pitcher bring out your can.

106

Get your fresh oysters from the Oyster Man ♪

We even had a man selling corn meal on the streets. The *Daily Delta* of June 3, 1850, reported the Corn Meal Man was doing business on horseback, and was noted for his wit and humor, as he prowled the streets of New Orleans. He would blow on a small brass trumpet, as he galloped through the streets while yelling, "*Bon jour, Madame, Mam-zelle!* Fresh corn meal right from the mill! *Oui, Mam-zelle!* Bring out your can and I will fill!" His greeting was accompanied by a hearty laugh.

To give a better idea of all the things that were sold on the street before corner groceries and long before super markets. New Orleans had street merchants that sold Flower, Charcoal, Clothes pole. (Before dryers, women hung clothes, on clothesline and the pole they bought for a nickel would keep the lineup, which would prevent the clothes from dragging near the ground after they were hung.) Then there was the vendor that sold brooms door to door. In addition, we had the Umbrella Man, the Waffle Man and of course, the Candy Man, which we still have today on St Charles Street.

In 1915, Sam Cortese had a wagon designed so he could make his mother's special Italian taffy recipe, as he rode through the streets of New Orleans. Sam's grandson, Ron Kottemann, uses the same wagon today, continuing a family business that long ago became a New Orleans tradition. He and his mule, Patsy, can be found rambling down the streets of the city and parking here and there, under the shade of an old oak tree. They have no set itinerary, so catching sight of them is always a surprise. For children exiting school at 3 o'clock, there aren't many things to make them happier. Finding the Roman Candy Man parked on the street outside of their school is always quite a surprise. He waits for the children to gather around his wagon to choose their favorite flavor. Mom and dad are usually very pleased also.

Roman candy was originally an Italian Taffy that had no flavor. It has been passed down through four generations of Italians from Sicily and was originally created for cleaning one's teeth. This was long before toothbrushes were invented.

NEW ORLEANS MILK MAN

Most of the older folks today can remember the milkman, who delivered milk in glass bottles with a thin cardboard cap on top, in the wee hours of the morning. He would place bottles of milk on the steps or porch by the front door and no one ever bothered them. How many bottles of milk a family wanted delivered that day, was easy for the milkman to figure out. If a family wanted two bottles, or maybe four, the milkman would see the empty bottles left outside by the front door. He would then replace the empties with the fresh bottles of milk. If he were to collect for his milk that day, the lady of the house, would simply leave a check, or cash in an envelope, that was stuck in one of the empty bottles. (How times have changed.) In New Orleans, the milkman delivering milk in glass bottles probably ended when families began moving out to the suburbs in the twentieth century.

110

Fresh milk and buttermilk were sold on the street from horse–drawn wagons long before the modern milkmen and glass bottles. The *Daily Picayune* in 1900, described the milk cart, as a tall high-wheeled wagon. It was usually driven by a "Garcon" (Young Man) who rang a bell to let the residents in the area know he was out front. The house wives would then come out of their homes to meet the milkman.

111

They had to supply their own containers. The wagon carried two large brassbound cans that ornamented the front of the wagon, compelling the driver to stand up much of the time in order to see clearly in front of him.

What is very interesting in the early life of our New Orleans Creole city, even water was sold in this fashion. So, selling water is not a 20th, or 21st Century innovation. Wine too was also peddled this way.

We must not forget the char-coal man that was very busy all year long traveling around the city delivering coal from his old broken down-wagon and being pulled by an equally broken-down horse. From the very beginning, every New Orleans housewives had to buy char-coal to heat water (outdoors of course), to fill their wash tubs with hot water in order to wash their clothes. Of course once the hot water heater began to be installed in homes, and washing machines became popular, the char-coal man ceased to exist. But, the wonderful creative sounds of this free man of color will never faded from our city as long as there are books to describe what he wrote and sang to bring the customers, with their buckets, to his wagon to get 25¢ worth of char-coal.

Char-coal lady! Char-coal lady!

My horse is white, my face is black

112

I sell my char-coal, two-bits a sack

Char-coal lady! Char-coal lady!

Also, in today's twenty-first century, recycling is very big around the country. Well, the *Daily Picayune,* July 12, 1891, described how nearly every week thirty or forty boats visited plantations above and below the city to collect bottles. They would then unload their cargo of old bottles at the wharves in New Orleans. Many dealers would employ collectors to pick up those bottles, because there was always a good market for beer bottles, whiskey and champagne bottles, and other bottles of all sorts. Medicine bottles were never resold

On the streets, the bottle man would go around from neighborhood to neighborhood to collect bottles and rags, which he resold. In addition, let's not forget the Junk man who went through the city picking up scrap iron, pieces of furniture and anything that he may feel was valuable.

Something else I'd like to mention about the uniqueness of New Orleans, is the snowball. It was mentioned in the YAT dictionary, but I'll explain it in more detail here. It is totally different from the watery, crunchy snow cones that are sold in other parts of the country. The New Orleans sno'balls are some of the most

113

elegant treats ever created, and are ridiculously simple yet habit-forming. The ingenious snowball machine was invented in New Orleans around 1934. The machine transforms a block of ice into mounds of delicate fluffy snow--like flakes, unlike the crunchy ice crystals from a snow cone machine. After ordering a snowball, you get to choose from up to 80 flavors offered at some snowball shops. Eventually the spelling was shortened to "sno'ball" by the locals. (It's a New Orleans thing.)

How did it all begin?

Well, to quote Rod Serling. "Picture this if you will" It's the late 1800's on a hot summer evening when adults and children came outside to sit on their steps. Their plan is to catch a cool breeze that might be blowing. In many parts of the city, you will find them waiting for the Snowball Man. He peddles shaved ice that he creates from a small hand scraper over which he would pour your choice of his delicious syrup. Where he got his block of ice back then has been lost in history.

The Snowball Man charged three to five cents and for an extra penny, you can get two kinds of syrup. The syrup was made with real flavoring. Back then, there weren't any such thing as extracts. There were delicious vanilla strawberry, raspberry, spearmint, chocolate, pineapple, orange, lemon and nectar syrups to choose from. Most

Snowball Men in the city traveled in every neighborhood using pushcarts.

Today the snowball pushcarts are gone. Now, there are snowball stands located in just about every section of the city and beyond. People will walk to their nearest stand to get their snowball. The snowball in today's world will cost 75 cents to two dollars and even more, depending on the size you order. At all snowball stands, you will be able to choose any of the many different flavors they have in their shop. For an extra twenty-five cents they will pour condense milk on top to make the snowball even more delicious.

Anyone who tends to eat their delicious snowball too fast is guaranteed a "Brain Freeze." Ask anyone who has ever had one. It evokes laughter from everyone present. Then when someone else succumbs to a "Brain Freeze," the laughter may start again, including the person who has it.

CHAPTER EIGHT

In the above chapter, we covered many areas of interest that was uniquely New Orleans at one time. As it was mentioned in the beginning, once some of our unique traditions and customs became popular with our wonderful tourists, they were adapted and used in other parts of the country. However, in the next chapter, the traditions that are listed, to the best of my knowledge, are exclusively preformed in and around New Orleans and nowhere else in the country. Once you read what those traditions are, you will understand why they were never adopted and used anywhere else.

EXCLUSIVE TRADITIONS ONLY IN NEW ORLEANS

ALL SAINTS DAY – November 1st

Even though All Saints Day is observed in many parts of the United States, it became "exclusive" in New Orleans by the way it was celebrated. Decorating the cemeteries on All Saints Day has been a New Orleans custom since the city's first cemetery opened in 1742. More widely observed than any other place in America, this custom continues, although somewhat more subdued in today's world. In times past, entire families gathered at the cemetery of their deceased relatives. In New Orleans, it was like a holiday. Everyone in the family would go the tomb to clean, paint and repair whatever was needed. They brought food and drinks and took a break from their labor, to have lunch right in the cemetery. After the tombs were completed, a bouquet of flowers was placed on the tomb. Some families would do this work a day or two ahead of time, so that on the morning of November 1st, the cemeteries were a magnificent sight to behold. Each tomb glistened white in the sun, with flowers everywhere, as far as the eye could see. Religious services were held in the cemeteries on that special family day.

All the families inside of the cemetery took tremendous pride in cleaning and decorating their family tombs. It was their way of honoring those who had gone before them.

The pictures above are from the 1930's and early 1940's.

When the crowd began to be as big as they were, and the entrepreneurial spirit being what it was in New Orleans, it wasn't long before vendors of all kinds began selling their wares just outside of the cemetery gates. There were vendors that sold flowers; some sold cleaning supplies, while others sold toys and candy for children. The atmosphere outside the cemetery was very festive at times. It became obvious to everyone living in New Orleans, that it was a public holiday

120

Now, we will end this section with the information that most people today may not know about New Orleans Saints Football Team.

On November 1, 1966, "All Saints Day" the New Orleans football team was formally admitted to the NFL. Therefore, the owner of the team approached then Archbishop Hannan and asked if it would be sacrilegious to use the word "Saints" for their football team, being that the team was admitted to the NFL on All Saints Day, November 1st at a league meeting on that day. Archbishop Hannan not only loved the idea, he wrote an official prayer for the team within that year. That is how our New Orleans Saints Football team got its name. (This information was taken from the New Orleans archdiocesan paper, the Clarion Herald, 1967.)

AS WE SAID EARLIER
ONLY IN NEW ORLEANS

BELOW YOU WILL FIND EVEN MORE THINGS THAT WERE EXCLUSIVLY NEW ORLEANS

There are at least few more traditions that were exclusively New Orleans, but no more. The first one many locals will still remember is "Manuel's Hot Tamales." They were sold on street corners throughout the city. There were "Hot Tamale" wagons on busy street corners throughout New Orleans at one time. As the years went by, there weren't as many wagons selling on street corners, but you could still buy the famous tamales at their shop on Carrollton Ave. Then, a sad thing happened; Hurricane Katrina destroyed their place of business. Sad, because Manuel Hernandez came from Mexico and started the tamale business in 1932. His famous hot tamales were loved by everyone who tasted them. Manuel's Hot Tamales has now passed on into culinary history. However, they will never be forgotten because they were made with the best of ingredients.

NEW ORLEANS PRALINES

The next tradition that was exclusively New Orleans is our famous pralines. The idea for the confection called praline came to New Orleans over 200 years ago. In France, a chef created almonds coated with boiled sugar, as a treat for a French diplomat by the name of Cesar Du Plessis Praslin. The name Praslin eventually evolved into "praline." A French immigrant brought the recipe to New Orleans in the 17th century. Because almonds were unavailable in Louisiana, pecans were substituted and cream was added. At that time, any recipe that didn't call for cream or butter was eyed with a certain amount of suspicion.

It wasn't long after that; a New Orleans tradition was born. Long before the Civil War, pralines became an early entrepreneurial endeavor for free women of color in New Orleans. An article in the *Daily Picayune* in 1900 described the old praline women who sold pralines on the streets of the French Quarter, in Jackson Square and on Canal Street. The paper described the women as being dressed in gingham, starched aprons with head raps. In the summer months, they would fan their candies with palmetto leaves to keep them cool. This was done while singing out "savoureux pralines - savoureux pralines" (tasty pralines – tasty pralines) to people passing by. That dainty French confection has delighted New Orleanians and our wonderful tourist for generations and will continue to do so as long as there is a New Orleans

JIM'S FRIED CHICKEN

Jim's Fried Chicken was exclusively New Orleans and was absolutely the best fried chicken in America back in the late 40's, 50's and early 1960.s. Mr. Jim started frying his chicken in New Orleans long before Colonel Sanders, or Popeye's Chicken became popular in our city and even after they existed, Jim's fried chicken was still the best. Jim's fried chicken was so delicious that people driving into their parking lot would have to wait about five or ten minutes after turning on their parking lights. As soon as she could, the carhop would come over to your car and take your order. Then, you would have to wait another 30 to 45 minutes before she brought it out to you on a metal tray that hooked onto your car door. Now, no one ever minded the wait, because it was customary to not go alone. You would always go with your date and while you are waiting, you would be doing a little smooching. In reality, (Chicken Jim) as all the teenagers call it back then, became a mild form of lover's lane. Everyone enjoyed four things about going to Chicken Jim's. 1. melt in your mouth fried chicken, which was crispy on the outside. 2. brought to your car piping hot on a tray with cold drinks. 3. The most enjoyable time of your life with your date, while waiting to eat your chicken. 4. Chicken Jim was always open all night, so after a night of bar hopping, drinking and dancing, before you would take your date home in the wee hours in the morning, it was customary for the hungry ones, to go to Chicken Jim and enjoy their date and the best fried chicken ever. Unfortunately, Chicken Jim is closed now.

Furthermore, this is interesting. Once Jim's Fried Chicken announce that they were closing, they had numerous requests from a lot of restaurants, (Too numerous to list here) to sell them their secret recipe, because no one was ever able to duplicate their melt in your mouth crispy fried chicken. The owners, who were the descendants of Mr. Jim the creator of the recipe made a decision to never sell the recipe in honor of Mr. Jim. Myself as well as many of us who enjoyed that fried chicken and the way we had to wait, do indeed honor the wishes of Mr. Jim's relatives.   Actually, the reason why we had to wait for such a long time was because of two reasons. One, because they were always very busy, and two, they never started frying your chicken until you gave the carhop your order. Your chicken came out freshly fried, rather than hot from a heat lamp, because it was cooked earlier, as it is done today at other chicken places.

125

FONG'S CHINESE RESTURANT

While eating out late in the wee hours of the morning, I have to mention a couple of more places we used to go before we took our date's home. One was Fong's Chinese restaurant on Decatur Street in the French Quarter. This was truly an authentic Chinese restaurant where you ate real Chinese food cooked by a real Chinese man born and raised in China. The food was delicious and the service was excellent. What's interesting, is that they didn't have waitresses, or waiters. The cook who prepared our food was the one who brought the food out to us. Then a little while after we began eating, the Chinese cook would come over to our table and ask us if we were enjoying our food. He wanted to make sure he prepared everything we ordered to suit our taste. One time I jokingly told the cook that the seaweed soup I ordered had sand in the bottom of the bowl. His eyes widened and stepped back and said to me. "Oh, I no cook that soup…..that was wife who cook soup…..I go back in kitchen and fuss at her. Give me bowl and I bring you soup I make."

After my friends and I laughed, I told Fong that I was only kidding and as usual, his seaweed soup was great tasting. We always enjoyed Fong's food, his restaurant and sometimes the music on the jukebox. They only had

Chinese music on the records and it only cost a nickel to play one of the songs. Everywhere else in New Orleans in the fifties and sixties, the juke box music you played was three for a quarter.

Once again, I must say.

ONLY IN NEW ORLEANS

As everyone knows, New Orleans has some of the best food in the country, so I have to mention one that was an exclusive to our city until Chefs around the country tasted one of the most delicious Italian sandwiches ever created the "Muffuletta." It is one of the great sandwiches of the world. It is also a bit of a lesson to those who think that the only cultural and culinary heritage of New Orleans is French, Spanish, African and Creole. If you ask anyone about the quintessential sandwiches of New Orleans, many people, tourist and locals alike will immediately say the "Po'boy." However, the Muffuletta is as New Orleans as any po'boy you'll ever eat and there's nothing Creole about it. The Muffuletta is pure Italian and pure Sicilian if you want to be specific. New Orleans, in its population and its cuisine, owes much to Italians and Sicilians who have been settling in the Crescent City since the middle 1800's and we are the richer for it.

127

The Muffuletta sandwich was created by Signor Lupo Salvadore, who opened the now famous Italian market called Central Grocery on Decatur Street in the French Quarter back in 1906. When I was growing up the Muffuletta was pronounced "Moo-foo-LET-ta, but for some reason, in modern times, a lot of people in New Orleans pronounce the sandwich "Muff-uh-LOT-uh," which is wrong. If only they would look at the spelling, they would see that "LET" is not Pronounced "LOT." Anyway, only in New Orleans, regardless how it's pronounced, all the Italian sandwich aficionados all agree that the Muffuletta is the best tasting Italian sandwich ever created.

Another exclusive food from New Orleans is of course our Gumbo which was created right here in our city. Right now, you can travel all over the country and find restaurants that claim to sell New Orleans gumbo. However, unless the chef was born and raised here, or came down here to learn the fine art of cooking our filé (pronounced Fee-lay), or seafood gumbo, I hardly think that what was made would be considered real New Orleans Creole gumbo. Of course, all throughout Louisiana and parts of Mississippi, you will defiantly find our New Orleans gumbo being made. Let me say that although it all began here in New Orleans, many area of

Louisiana, such as the Cajuns in and around Acadiana are known to create an exceptionally delicious gumbo which is slightly different, but just as good as our New Orleans Creole gumbo. However, I must admit that even in New Orleans, almost every family in and around our city will cook their gumbo slightly different.

The reason why I'm mentioning that, is because I want to clarify why the cooking of gumbo, even though it is done differently even within the same family, it is still a New Orleans creation and the taste is unbeatable. The bottom line is that the Creole gumbo that was created in our city, has spread out over the past 200 plus years to all parts of Louisiana and all points east and west of New Orleans.

Something else that is exclusively found only in New Orleans is our original type of Mardi Gras celebration that is given every year. People from all over the world come to our city for the largest free show in the country. A lot of small cities and towns throughout Louisiana celebrate Mardi Gras, but New Orleans is the largest. Plus Mardi Gras Food choices are steeped in tradition with one great indispensable dish: The King Cake. The Mardi Gras season begins on the feast of the Epiphany (January 6) which commemorates the arrival of the three wise men (The Kings) and culminates with the final bash on what we call Fat Tuesday (Mardi Gras Day).

129

It was in our city that the King Cake was created, so leading up to Mardi Gras day, people all over the city would get together and have King Cake parties. The King Cake is a ring of twisted sweet bread topped with colored icing of purple, green and gold (The traditional Mardi Gras colors). Now today, a lot of bakeries fill their King Cakes with different types of fillings. Much of the fun at the King Cake parties is waiting to see who will get the tiny plastic baby hidden inside the cake. Tradition has it that whoever gets the slice of cake with the baby inside, is crowned Mardi Gras King and must then host the next Mardi Gras King Cake party. This will continue until the final day of the celebration, Mardi Gras day which is Fat Tuesday. The next day of course is Ash Wednesday which is the beginning of Lent, this is the time when all Catholics make plans to give up something they enjoy, until Easter Sunday. Now, anyone reading this and want to know more about the solemn Lenten tradition, should go to Google and type in Lent, and you will get the full story.

THE NEW ORLEANS LUCKY BEAN

I have to mention another Catholic-derived tradition that falls during Lent that is exclusively New Orleans and its suburbs. It is the "Saint Joseph altar," originally a custom of Italian families and parishes that have become woven into the culture of our greater New Orleans life along with the New Orleans lucky bean.

On March 19, the Roman Catholic feast day of Saint Joseph, almost 50 churches in the Archdiocese of New Orleans will open their doors for parishioners and guests to view the ornate three-tiered altars. They feature devotional items and mounds of food that will be blessed by a priest and distributed to the needy.

The elaborate decorative arrangements of food and other offerings began on the Italian island of Sicily during the middle ages. In the midst of a drought that caused a severe famine, island residents began eating fava beans – otherwise used as animal feed. When all their other crops failed they began praying to Saint Joseph to intercede for an end to the drought. Agriculture was very important to the island and for a very long time, there had been no rain to nourish the crops. The dried out wheat stalks cracked beneath the feet of the poor farmers as they walked through their barren fields. Only a sea of dust and withered vines remained for what had once been rows and rows of brightly colored fruits and vegetables. The only thing that thrived was the fava bean. The situation was critical. At that time during the Middle Ages, many countries were having their own problems. So, with no help from the outside world, the Sicilians began surviving by eating the fava bean.

After a lot of praying to St. Joseph their patron saint for relief from the terrible famine that gripped the island, the skies finally opened up, sending down the life-given water to survive. The people rejoiced. Later, to show their gratitude, they prepared a table in their homes with a large assortment of foods that they were able to harvest. That was to pay homage to St. Joseph for helping them survive. After paying honor to St Joseph, the Sicilians who were able to set up their tables of food, then decided to distribute all the food to the less fortunate around the island.

The following year all across Sicily people began building St. Joseph Altars in their homes as a way of giving thanks to St Joseph for the blessing of a bountiful harvest. They would usually have a family thanksgiving dinner to give thanks to St. Joseph that the famine came to an end and their people survived. After the participants enjoyed their meal, all the families who set up St. Joseph Altars, would give all the food that was placed on the altar to the poor and unfortunate. It became a meatless altar, because the Sicilians had no meat during the famine. Everyone was given a fava bean which soon became known as the "Lucky Bean." It became the symbol of "abbondanza," the abundances of sharing in the blessings of faith, hope and love.

When the Sicilians came to New Orleans in the late 1800's, they brought their tradition of building St. Joseph Altars with them.   The large concentration of Sicilian Immigrants in New Orleans explains why this tradition is almost exclusive in and around our city.   While most Italian immigrants from Naples settled in New York and other cities along the eastern seaboard, the Sicilians sailed from Palermo and landed in New Orleans.   What's interesting is that between 1850 and 1870, the U.S. Census Bureau estimated that there were more Italians in New Orleans than any other U.S. city.   By 1910, the population of the city's French Quarter was 80% Italian. Then up until Hurricane Katrina, there were well over 200,000 Americans of Italian descent living in New Orleans and its suburbs, making Italian Americans the largest ethnic group in the city.   When you consider that the entire metropolitan area was around 700,000 inhabitants that meant that about 29% of all the people in the area were of Italian descent. Therefore, because of the large Italian population in and around New Orleans, the St. Joseph Altar around March 19 of every year became a city wide celebration even for those who were not Italian. All over the city, people would take time out to visit the beautiful St. Joseph altars with its large assortments of food. Of course no one is ever allowed to eat the food off of the altar, because traditionally, all the food which has

133

been blessed by a priest is meant for the unfortunate and the very poor Those who visit the St. Joseph altars are the given a little bag. In that bag is a St. Joseph prayer card, a piece of Italian bread that's been blessed, some Italian cookies and a blessed fava bean (Lucky Bean).

Although the last item explicitly links the celebration with its Sicilian roots, it is widely known as the "New Orleans Lucky Bean." Hopefully, this will explain why the "Lucky Bean" has found its way into the purses and pockets of many and is kept as a treasured memento of the St. Joseph's Feast Celebration. Some believe if their pantry contains a fava (lucky bean) it will never be bare and will always have enough food for the family and anyone who keeps a lucky bean it their purse or pocket will never be broke.

Many people in New Orleans will admit to you that they carry a St. Joseph Lucky Bean with them. And if you ask them, they will tell you where it came from and why they considered it lucky. Needless to say, because the "Lucky Bean" has such an interesting story, I felt that I should tell the whole story right here. After all, it is possible that most of the younger generation wouldn't even know how or why the fava bean that a lot of locals carry with them considers it a "New Orleans Lucky Bean."

I need to mention another exclusive story about New Orleans and the entire state of Louisiana. It is about Parishes as opposed to Counties in the rest of our United States. I thought I would mention it here, because there may be a lot of people around the country that do not know why we are the only state in the union that do not call the administration sub-division of a state a county. You see, when Louisiana belonged to France, the state was divided up by parishes. Then, when the United States bought the Louisiana territory, the state of Louisiana was allowed to remain under the Napoleonic Code that represented French law, while the other 49 states are strictly based on English Common Law. I hope that explains why we have parishes in Louisiana instead of counties.

ONE OF THE MANY THINGS THAT MAKE NEW ORLEANS A VERY INTERESTING CITY IS ITS PAST.

THE TRUE STORIES BELOW WILL VARIFY THAT.

Like no other city in the country, New Orleans had legalized dueling from the very beginning. There were a lot of stories throughout our history that will tell about the many interesting duels that took place in City Park under

135

the "Dueling Oaks." However, the one that I will mention below has got to be the most interesting story of all that concerns legalized duels, where one man challenges another. Believe it or not, hundreds of years later, the oak tree that men fought duel under is still there.

This is a true story about Captain S. M. Harvey, who was a very successful whaler and decided to retire while he was still a very young man in 1840. His plan was to leave his northern winters behind him, so after giving the matter due consideration, he chose New Orleans as his new home. He was welcomed and it didn't take long for him to become a prominent and popular member of the city's society. Not long after coming to New Orleans, Captain Harvey married Louise Destrehan, who was from a distinguished Louisiana family, then settled down to a serene and happy life.

It wasn't long before Captain Harvey's serenity and his life was threatened one day following an altercation during a card game at the home of a friend. He and another guest, Albert Farve, got into a heated discussion and action followed words when the Captain became provoked and punched Mr. Farve in the nose. Unfortunately, the Captain was not accustomed to the Creole way of life and the consequence that was involved in hitting someone in New Orleans in the 1800's.

An act such as that was considered a very high insult and a man who was accosted in this way would certainly demand satisfaction, usually in the form of either a sword fight, or pistols at twenty paces. Creole honor was a delicate thing and a man could be insulted over the most trivial of events, a word, or a look might end in a duel. In fact, more duels took place in New Orleans, than any other city in the country. In the early to mid-1800, hardly a day went by without at least one duel being fought. According to the *Daily Delta* one winter morning in 1839, there were ten consecutive duels beneath the ancient oak tree on the dueling grounds in City Park.

In the very early days, the St Anthony's Garden, behind the St. Louis Cathedral was used as a dueling site. But the priests complained of the "noise," so the duels were moved to the Allard plantation, which later became part of City Park. "Didn't the priest care about a killing?"

After the incident between Captain Harvey and Mr. Farve, it was no surprise that the next day Mr. Farve's appointed his second, who arrived at the Captain's home to deliver his challenge for a duel on the fields of honor. Captain Harvey felt that he had a nice life and wasn't very happy about the prospect of surrendering it his life over to something as trivial as a card game. He had no experience at dueling with either swords or pistols. Even worse, he knew without a doubt that Mr. Farve certainly did have the experience. The situation didn't look promising.

However, the Captain was made aware that by him refusing the challenge it would bring so much disgrace upon him and his family that he would probably be forced to leave town by everyone who knew him. Fortunately, the Captain was a man with a certain amount of ingenuity and he put that ingenuity to work.

The rules were simple. When a man challenges another to a duel, it is left to the person who'd been challenged to choose the weapon. Men who get involved in a duel have clashes with swords, pistols, shotguns and for some reason even with a poison pill. The way they do the poison pill sounds crazy. The men get a deck of cards and a drawing is held to determine which man will take the pill. (Sounds a bit like Russian roulette.)

The old dueling oak tree on the dueling ground in City Park had been witness to every conceivable type of weapon, or so one might have thought. Mr. Farve's second stood on Captain Harvey's doorstep that bright winter morning, waiting to learn what his choice of weapon might be. The second could not have guessed what he was about to hear. You can only imagine his astonishment when the Captain boldly announced, "Whaling harpoons!"

Immediately, Mr. Farve's second objected. How could a harpoon actually be considered a weapon? To answer the question, Captain Harvey led the second to his backyard. He picked up his harpoon, walked off twenty paces, turned and took aim at a small tree. The harpoon flew and found its mark dead center. The tree promptly split in half. The second, somewhat startled by marvelous exhibition, exclaimed, "What do you suppose my friend to be? A fish?" However, the Captain was unyielding and harpoons were the weapons that would be used.

The second left and of course immediately returned to his friend Mr. Farve and reported to him, the weapon of choice and the skill with which the Captain used the devise.

After thinking the matter over carefully, Mr. Farve decided that perhaps, after all, the insult wasn't as severe as first thought. "We will," he said to his second, "let bygones be bygones and not discuss the matter again." (An excellent example, if I ever heard one, of discretion being the better part of valor.)

CHAPTER NINE

I cannot close this book, without mentioning one of the great New Orleans characters that will live in our history forever. His name was Jean Lafitte! In this chapter I will tell you a little bit about this famous pirate who was also a patriot that was admired by everyone who knew him over a hundred years ago, including the president of the United States.

Lafitte and his men loved New Orleans and lived in the city from time to time, when they were not out in the Caribbean attacking Spanish ships. Many of his men married as well as his brother Pierre who had children and centuries later the descendants still live in New Orleans.

Pierre's blacksmith shop still exists in New Orleans on the corner of Bourbon and St. Philip Street, which was built in 1772. Today is being used as a bar/nightclub. Below is a picture of what it looks like today.

I need to show another ancient building in the New Orleans French Quarter that involved Jean Lafitte. Few buildings have been pictured more, or had as many stories told about it than the old plastered-brick building on the corner of Bourbon and Bienville Streets. Inside, according to legend, it had a secret staircase with rooms upstairs where General Andrew Jackson and Pirate Jean Lafitte planned the strategy for the battle of 1812 in Chalmette. They spent long hours plotting a way to defeat the British and save the city of New Orleans.

The Legend of Jean Lafitte

Jean Lafitte was a handsome man with hazel eyes and dark hair. He was well over six feet in height and very muscular. Whenever he walked the streets of old New Orleans where he called home, no one would ever dared challenge him. He was soft-spoken and very polite. However everyone knew he could be very dangerous if he became angered. He had absolute influence over his men whether they were on shore or at sea, as he preyed upon the shipments of Spanish gold in the Caribbean.

While living in New Orleans, Jean Lafitte established a partnership with his brother Pierre in the operation of a blacksmith shop around 1809 located on the corner of Bourbon and St Philip Street. Actually it was a front for selling pirate's loot. They did so well, they decided to open a store on Royal Street. They felt that having a nice storefront for their ill-gotten pirate goods would look better for the planters and merchants who bought from them.

When the British planned to attack New Orleans in the war of 1812, they offered Lafitte money and a commission of Captain in the Royal Navy if he would fight with them against the United States. He refused and instead offered his service with his unscrupulous crew to General Jackson in the defense of New Orleans, the city he loved. Jean Lafitte and his men fought with such great

143

fighting spirit to defeat the British, General Jackson cited them for bravery and President Madison gave each man a pardon after the war

However, after the battle of New Orleans, Jean Lafitte decided to return to the sea and soon passed into legend. It is said that at his peak, strong men feared him and the mere mention of his name made lovely maidens swoon.

Because he and his band of scoundrels fought bravely in the defense of New Orleans, he has earned a place in American history. With one act of heroism, we in our city of New Orleans tend to overlook the countless crimes of one of the most feared pirate in the Caribbean.

A soldier of fortune, privateer, pirate and defender of our city, Jean Lafitte will live in history as the most patriotic scamp that ever unfurled his black flag with its skull and crossbones, wielded a cutlass and plundered for "pieces of eight."

Well, you have just read all about one of the most unique cities in our country, or maybe even the world. Regardless of our heritage, we are all part of a very large family that has existed in and around New Orleans from the very beginning. Absolutely every nationality that calls this city home has contributes to the food, the speech, the fun and the celebrations that we so willing share with the outside world.

THE END

If anyone needs more information about our city,

I can be reached at Italian77740@gmail.com